ALMOST A CHRISTIAN
by Matthew Mead
with chapters by C. Matthew McMahon

Copyright Information

Almost A Christian, by Matthew Mead, with chapters by C. Matthew McMahon
Edited by Therese B. McMahon

Copyright ©2019 by Puritan Publications and A Puritan's Mind®

Some language and grammar has been updated from the original manuscript. Any change in wording or punctuation has not changed the intent or meaning of the original author(s), and has been made to aid the modern reader in gently updated language.

Published by Puritan Publications
A Ministry of A Puritan's Mind® in Crossville, TN
www.apuritansmind.com
www.puritanpublications.com

All rights reserved. No part of this publication may be reproduced, stored in a retrieval system or transmitted in any form by any means, electronic, mechanical, photocopy, recording or otherwise, without the prior permission of the publisher, except as provided by USA copyright Law.

This Print Edition, 2019
Electronic Edition, 2019
Manufactured in the United States of America

ISBN: 978-1-62663-325-4
eISBN: 978-1-62663-324-7

Table of Contents

Meet Matthew Mead 4

The False Professor 9

Original Title Page 21

To the Hearers 22

To the Reader 26

Introduction 33

Question 1 48

Question 2 122

Question 3 127

Question 4 139

Question 5 148

Application 156

Use of Examination 160

Use of Caution 170

Use of Exhortation 182

Other Helpful Works by Matthew Mead at Puritan Publications 203

Meet Matthew Mead
Compiled by C. Matthew McMahon

Matthew Mead (or Meade) (1630-1699) was born about 1630 at Leighton Buzzard, Bedfordshire. He was an independent divine, second son of Richard Mead of Mursley, Buckinghamshire. His tombstone inscription accordingly speaks of him as *one honest among his family*.

In 1648 he was elected as a scholar in Cambridge, and on August 11, 1649 admitted as a fellow of King's College. He resigned that post on June 6, 1651 to avoid expulsion concerning certain political problems with the faculty.

Mead became *morning* lecturer at Stepney Church (St. Bunstan's), where the *afternoon* lecturer was William

Greenhill. Mead resided in Gracechurch Street, and was admitted as a member on December 28, 1656, of the congregational church formed at Stepney by Greenhill in 1644. On January 22, 1658 he was appointed by Oliver Cromwell to the "new chapel" at Shadwell (at St. Paul's). From Shadwell, as well as from his lectureship, he was ejected at the *Restoration* of Charles II, but obtained a lectureship at St. Sepulchre's, Holborn, from which he was again ejected by the *Act of Uniformity* in 1662.

In 1663 he lived at Worcester House, Stepney. Either the *Conventicle Act* (1664) or the *Five Miles Act*, which came into operation in 1660, drove him to Holland. He seems to have been in London during the great plague of 1665. On January 31, 1669 he was called to exercise his gifts as an assistant to William Greenhill at Stepney. He accepted the call on February 21. Shortly after Greenhill's death he was called to succeed him as pastor, and was ordained on December 14, 1671 by John Owen, D.D., Joseph Caryl, and two others. In 1674 a meeting-house was built for him at Stepney which was opened on September 13. The roof of this new meeting house was upheld by four round pine pillars, "presented to him by the States of Holland." Above the ceiling was an attic with a concealed entrance, a hiding place for the congregation in troubled times. Mead's congregation was the largest in London due to his excellent preaching of the Word of God, and droves of people from all over the city, and from afar, came to hear him preach.

About 1680 Mead became the guardian of James Peirce, the Exeter heretic, who lived in his house for some years. In December 1682 Sir William Smith, with a strong guard invaded his meeting-house, pulled down the pulpit, and broke up the forms. In June 1683 Mead was apprehended on suspicion of complicity in the *Rye House* plot, and brought before the privy council, when his answers were so satisfactory that the king at once ordered his discharge. He succeeded John Owen in September of 1683 as one of the Tuesday morning lecturers (Presbyterian and congregational) at the merchants' lecture in Pinners' Hall.

In 1686 Mead was again in Holland, preaching at Utrecht; he returned on the issue of King James' declaration for liberty of conscience in 1687.

After the revolution, in 1690, a movement began by John Howe in an attempt to join the Presbyterian and Congregationalist bodies. Mead was partial to this joint effort. The "happy union" held its meeting at Stepney on April 6, 1691, when Mead preached his famous sermon, "Two Sticks made One" on Ezek. 37:19. On the rupture of the union (in 1694) through the alleged heresies of Daniel Williams, D.D., Mead took a moderate part, but remained in the Pinners' Hall lectureship when the Presbyterians seceded. When Edmund Calamy applied to him (in 1694) for ordination he declined to act, from no scruples of his own, but for fear of giving umbrage to others. He preached his last sermon in May 1699, and died on October 16, 1699, at age 70. He was buried in Stepney churchyard. John Howe preached his funeral sermon. He is described as a *gentleman and a scholar.*

His works are:

Besides separate sermons, 1660-98, including funeral sermons for Thomas Rosewell (1692) and Timothy, he published:

1. "The Almost Christian Discovered," *etc.*, 1662, 8vo (substance of sermons at St. Sepulchre's, Holborn, in 1661); often reprinted; in Dutch, Utrecht, 1682, 12mo; in Welsh, Merthyr Tydfil, 1825, 12mo; *this current volume.*
2. "Solomon's Prescription for the Removal of the Pestilence," *etc.*, 1666, 4to; 1667, 12mo (with appendix); (which has been published by *Puritan Publications*).
3. "The Good of Early Obedience," *etc.*, 1683, 8vo (Mayday sermons).
4. "The Vision of the Wheels," Sec, 1689, 4to (sermons on Ezekiel, which have been published by *Puritan Publications*).

Posthumous works were:

5. "The Young Man's Remembrancer," *etc.*, 3rd edit. 1701, 8vo (his last two Mayday sermons; often reprinted).
6. "Original Sermons on the Jews; and on Falling into the Hands of God with a Memoir," *etc.*, 1836, 12mo (edited from shorthand notes transcribed by James Andrews in 1703 and 1710; the manuscripts, long preserved in the family of Sir Thomas W. Blomefield, bart., are now in the British Museum). He had a hand in the "English Greek Lexicon," 1661 8vo. His farewell sermon before ejection was published separately, 1662, 4to and 12mo, and also in the "Compleat Collection," 1663, 8vo. He wrote a preface to "The Life and Death of Nathaniel Mather," 1689, 8vo. In earlier documents

he spelled his name "Meade," but used the spelling "Mead" from about 1679. Three engraved portraits of him are known.

For further study:

Funeral Sermon by John Howe 1699; Calamy's *Account*, 1713, p. 471; Calamy's *Continuation*, 1727, ii. 614; Calamy's *Own Life*, 1830, i. 142, 341 sq.; Walker's *Sufferings of the Clergy*, 1714, ii. 215, 260; Feirce's *Vindication of the Dissenters*, 1718, i. 258; Peirce's *Remarks*, 1719, p. 42; *Protestant Dissenter's* Magazine, 1799, p. 140; Palmer's *Nonconformist's Memorial*, 1802, ii. 461 sq.; Wilson's *Dissenting Churches of London*, 1808, ii. 252, 1810, iii. 31; Toulmin's *Historical View*, 1814, p. 104; Neal's *Hist., of the Puritans* (Toulmin), 1822, v. 37; Urwick's *Nonconformity in Hertfordshire*, 1884, p. 647; Jones's *Notes on the Early Days of Stepney Meeting* [1887]; *Hist. MSS. Comm.* 3rd Sep. App. x. 269; Cole's manuscript *Hist, of King's College, Cambridge*, iii. 201 sq.; *A Booke for Church Affaires at Stepny* (folio manuscript records from 1644 to present time).

The False Professor
by C. Matthew McMahon, Ph.D.

What is a *false professor?* It has nothing to do with a deceitful teacher in a college. It is not about college academia at all. Interestingly, Matthew Mead's work originally included in the title "The False Professor Tried and Cast." Being a false professor, is really being a counterfeit Christian. It is one who professes Christ, without having the true grace of the Holy Spirit and the redemption wrought by Christ in a born-again heart. It is one who acts outwardly one way which is internally opposed by the Gospel and all manner of true religion.

Scripturally speaking, there is no phrase "false professor," in the Bible, just as there is no phrase "triune Godhead," or, "Trinity," in the Bible. The term "false professor" is really a practical and theological term packed with biblical application concerning someone who *claims* the Christian faith saying "I am a good Christian," without being affected by any of the real qualities of Christian grace in their heart or life. A false professor is one that thinks they are part of the Christian crowd, and they may be just that – part of the earthly crowd – but not of the heavenly crowd; one who has never really been converted or has never really dealt with their sin at the mercy seat of the Savior.

In countless passages the Bible makes a dichotomy between those saved and lost, but it also makes a dichotomy between those who are the *presumingly* saved and the truly saved. This second comparison is set in the context of the covenanted, visible church, and it makes a clear distinction between the sheep and the goats, both of which exist *in* the church of God until the end of time. They are not now separated, one from the other, but instead, as Christ directs, will be separated at the last day. "When the Son of man shall come in his glory, and all the holy angels with him, then shall he sit upon the throne of his glory: And before him shall be gathered all nations: and he shall separate them one from another, as a shepherd divideth his sheep from the goats: And he shall set the sheep on his right hand, but the goats on the left," (Matt. 25:31-33). This will be a most terrible time of judgment where many who *thought* they were saved, and did great *works* in the name of Christ, will be told by Christ, "I profess unto them, I never knew you: depart from me, ye that work iniquity," (Matt. 7:22-23). One shudders, now, about the horror of it all.

The notion of the false professor is not attached to those who are merely pagan and lost, *i.e.* those of the world. The phrase is attached to religious *hypocrisy, those in the church*. False professors are hypocrites, attesting to the Christian faith, attempting to work religious works in their own strength, and are really *pretending* to get into the kingdom of heaven. The very word "hypocrite" means "pretender." They might even begin well in the Christian life, from a *human* vantage point, but finish most horribly, shipwrecking any ounce of faith they might have thought they had, "which some having put away concerning faith have made shipwreck," (1 Tim. 1:19).

Do you profess Christ but do not really know if you are saved? Or, maybe you profess Christ and think you *are* saved, but have not entered into a time of biblical reflection to discern whether or not you are in fact redeemed *by Christ*. Sometimes this can be a difficult question to work through. Often, sanguine people would like to think of themselves as Christians – maybe they equate a Christian with being subjectively morally good? People often like to categorized themselves as *moral*, or at least *more moral* than the next guy. But the, "I'm more moral than the next guy," theology never works. You might think you are more moral than Harry next door; but Harry next door might be a secret serial killer who thinks he is more moral than Stalin. And Stalin might think he was more moral than Hitler. And Hitler might think he is more moral than Judas. You get the picture. Though people are not inherently moral in the way God prescribes (which is to be *perfect*),[1] they still, at some level, *think they are.* I think at least most religiously lost people would believe that. Surely, there are the atheists and agnostics who openly *hate* Jesus Christ and simply use such philosophical systems to hide their sin.[2] Yet, for the most part, people would like to think of themselves as basically good people – especially all those who attend Evangelical churches today throughout Christendom. They have no idea what it means to be a depraved sinner,[3] nor do they care to know.[4]

---

[1] "Be ye therefore perfect, even as your Father which is in heaven is perfect," (Matt. 5:48).
[2] "If ye were blind, ye should have no sin: but now ye say, We see; therefore your sin remaineth," (John 9:41).
[3] "And GOD saw that the wickedness of man was great in the earth, and that every imagination of the thoughts of his heart was only evil continually." (Gen. 6:5).
[4] "God is not in all his thoughts," (Psa. 10:4).

However, I didn't ask you if you thought you were basically good, rather, I'm asking you to consider your status in a head-on encounter with Jesus Christ and the biblical prescriptions for true godliness and salvation only found in him. Are *you* a Christian? Now I suppose here people have all sorts of ideas about what a "Christian" may be. But I don't want you to dive into all kinds of varying opinions. We don't much care about subjective opinions from either people in the church or in the world. What we are looking for initially is the positive response a person should have if they are a true follower of Jesus Christ, and they objectively know their Bibles – a supernatural experimental attestation of the objective reality that demonstrates the mind and will of God for every born again believer in both their character and conduct. When I ask you if you are a Christian, I am asking this in light of the teachings of Jesus Christ *himself.* You may say, "Well I am unsure of "all" the teachings of Jesus Christ." To a certain point, you have answered my question already. To disregard who Jesus Christ is, and what he taught, is to certainly place yourself in opposition to everything he is and everything he taught. It *may* be you are a new Christian and have not yet read your bible through enough times to know. Keep on the good path of reading it *daily.* But if you are a Christian for some length of years, then you should have read through your bible a number of times, and should be familiar with what Jesus Christ taught, and what God requires. Do you live up to that? True Christians are not content with just a little of God, or a little of Christ, or a little of the Spirit, or a little of the Word, *etc.* A false professor, a hypocrite, is a person who individually holds a *little* of what God teaches in the word, *but not too much*. They hold a bit of what Christ taught, a *little* religiosity, but will never over-do it as a holy roller. They will read a passage in their Bible, pray a bit, attend church services, be involved in some way in the church, and other duties that they think are profitable, and they will speak greatly about being "blessed" by God, just like the celebrities do on TV when they win an award. These church goers believe God loves them, is patient with them, blesses them, and they are thankful for it. But you will never hear them speaking about being *holy*, or conformed to *holiness*, or delighting in *holiness*, or being separate from the world in *holiness*. For, without, "holiness, ... no man shall see the Lord," (Heb. 12:14). No, such people will not have anything of *that*, nor do they know what *that* really means. They are confident that what they have is enough, and that they do not need any more than what they minimally have obtained. They have *enough* of religion and may very well be diligent in what they minimally do. However, they will not have, as Mr. Mead says, "the least dram of grace" in them.

    One cannot be indifferent to the teachings of Jesus Christ, or, as Jesus said, they will be in *opposition* to him. "He that is not with me is against me; and he that gathereth not with me scattereth abroad," (Matt. 12:30). There is no gray area here. In reality, Jesus Christ said that anyone who was either indifferent to him or opposed to him is essentially in the same boat. They are *against him* and *lost*. They are *lost* in a world of sin which is deceiving them about their true spiritual state. They are not taking the kingdom by violence,[5] they are not pressing into the kingdom,[6] they are not forsaking all, they are not soaking up a conformed holiness to the Lord,[7] and Christ is not *all in all* for them.[8]

Consider something a bit trivial, but important. Here is a partial list of names that have something religious in common. Some of them you may be familiar with, and others maybe not so much. Let's take a quick *quiz*. See if you, the *astute* reader, can figure out what all these people have in *common*.

> Jacob Arminius, Teacher in the 17th century.
> Karl Barth, Neo-liberal theologian.
> Billy Graham, Arminian Evangelist.
> Harry Emerson Fosdick, Liberalism's popularizer.
> G.K. Chesterton, Roman Catholic essayist, poet, and writer.
> T.S. Eliot, Modernist poet.
> William Miller, The Founder 7th Day Adventism.
> Ignatius of Loyola, Roman Catholic Founder of the Society of Jesus (the Jesuits).
> Catherine of Siena, Religious Mystic and political activist.

---

[5] "And from the days of John the Baptist until now the kingdom of heaven suffereth violence, and the violent take it by force." (Matt 11.12).
[6] "The law and the prophets were until John: since that time the kingdom of God is preached, and every man presseth into it," (Luke 16:16).
[7] "...to be conformed to the image of his Son," (Rom. 8:29).
[8] "...the fulness of him that filleth all in all," (Eph. 1:23).

Walter Rauschenbusch, Champion of the social gospel.

What do all these people have in common? They are, according to *Christian History Magazine*, part of the top 131 Christian people everyone should know about. Really? That's right, Walter Rauschenbusch, who is the champion of the social gospel, and T.S. Elliot the modernist's poet, and the Anti-Christian Roman Catholic founder of the Jesuits – Ignatius Loyola, are among those "Christians" that *Christian History Magazine* says you, the astute reader, should know. From their perspective, *shame on you* if you didn't get the answers right to this little quiz.

It seems, however, that the term "Christian" simply means someone who in Religious History has done or accomplished something noticeable by a great many people; it seems it covers the *popular vote* at some level. Maybe they wrote a book people read, or published a religious poem, or preached what some might consider a famous sermon, or even *founded a cult*. It seems that the word "Christian" has lost its biblical derivative – those that actually follow Jesus Christ and his teachings found in Scripture.

The 21st century Evangelical church thrives on its inclusivistic nature, (everyone is welcome, everyone is a Christian, everyone is accepted) where, on the other hand, Christ always said the *opposite*. Christ was an *exclusivist*.

The Gospel he preached was exclusive,[9] given to a few,[10] lavished on a remnant of chosen people,[11] those chosen by God,[12] to receive the implanted Word,[13] by which, that alone, is able to the save the soul through faith by the power of the Spirit of Grace in applying all of Christ's merits and work to the believer.[14] Yes, many are called, but *few* are chosen. Was Jesus a liar in this?

The modern church of our era has it quite backwards. Christians are not simply people who write religious books, or quaint poems, or even preach to a congregation of listeners each Sunday. Doing something religiously noticeable and drawing attention to one's religious work is *not*, nor *ever* the criteria for being *called a Christian*, much less being a *true* Christian.[15]

The false professor in all this is in eternal trouble. They have a limited time to correct their bearings, and they would do well to listen to Mr. Mead in his presentation of real spiritual examination. Truly, this work is *about* spiritual examination. It is to place under a microscope the *professing Christian*, to find out whether that Christian is

---

[9] "He answered and said unto them, Because it is given unto you to know the mysteries of the kingdom of heaven, but to them it is not given," (Matt. 13:11).
[10] "Because strait is the gate, and narrow is the way, which leadeth unto life, and few there be that find it," (Matt. 7:14).
[11] "Even so then at this present time also there is a remnant according to the election of grace," (Rom. 11:5).
[12] "For many are called, but few are chosen," (Matt. 22:14).
[13] "Wherefore lay apart all filthiness and superfluity of naughtiness, and receive with meekness the engrafted word, which is able to save your souls," (James 1:21).
[14] "Elect according to the foreknowledge of God the Father, through sanctification of the Spirit, unto obedience and sprinkling of the blood of Jesus Christ," (1 Peter 1:2).
[15] See my work, *5 Marks of a Biblical Disciple*.

a true believer, or they have merely deceived themselves being *almost a Christian.* What a terrible place to be before God as a false professor. This is to delude one's self for decades only to find out upon their last breath, at the judgment seat of God, that Christ "never knew you." Many souls miscarry into eternity on such grounds. Mead is not out to beat you down in this regard. He is not merely looking to scare you into some new conformity to Jesus Christ. He is not Bible thumping purely to beat his Bible on someone's brow. He has orderly and precisely laid out a series of biblical propositions and their corollary answers to help you discern, and thoroughly examine, your current spiritual state before Jesus Christ. It is a simple question he looks to answer. Are you truly in the faith, or have you deceived yourself?

    The title of this work, "Almost a Christian" is used by Mead through the pages of his treatise no less than 108 times. The book is *only* 200 pages. Every time you turn one full page, you'll find Mead using that phrase. That phrase is a *biblical* phrase. It is found in Mead's exegetical and yet, spring-boarded text. "Almost thou persuadest me to be a Christian," (Acts 26:28). This statement by Agrippa is the foundation on which the entire treatise revolves. What does it mean to be "almost a Christian?" This is, as Mead will explain, no doubt, one of the saddest positions that any person can be in within the bounds of an earthly experience. *How far* can a man or woman go, *how far* can a teenager or child go in the profession of following Jesus Christ, and yet, after everything is considered, and their lives are over, and they stand before the Judge of the earth, that they actually *fall short of salvation?* How far may a man, woman, or child run the race of the Christian, and yet *not run* as to obtain their end? What a most terrible thought, and sad consequence, of so many people throughout history that have entered eternity unaware of their present danger. It is a *most sad consequence* to their graceless life that they enter into eternity to find the answer, when it is too late, and the day of Christ's grace has passed.

As all good puritans, Mead lays this treatise out on a singular text, and a singular doctrine, yet, radically expounded into a number of helpful points. His doctrine is this, "There are very many in the world that are almost, and yet but almost Christians; many that are near heaven, and yet are never the nearer; many that are within a little of salvation, and yet shall never enjoy the least salvation; they are within sight of heaven, and yet shall never have a sight of God." His goal is to bring false professors into being *altogether Christians*, instead of *almost a Christian*. He wants to see a real spiritual change in people for the glory of God.

In the course of the work, he will cover five questions, in which he answers them almost exhaustively, but precisely and concisely.

1. How far a man may go in the way to heaven, and yet be but *almost a Christian*.
2. Where it is that a man goes so far as to be *almost a Christian*.
3. If a natural conscience may go so far, then what difference is there between this natural conscience in hypocrites and sinners, and a renewed conscience in believers?

4. When is it that a man is *almost a Christian*, and when he has gone only so far.

5. What is the reason men go no further in religion, then to be *almost Christians?*

After successfully dealing with the five questions, he applies the doctrine, and then gives "uses" as a result of the application. The uses are biblical *gold*. Take your time in dealing with them for your spiritual profit.

Before you begin, take note, it was not Mead's intention to rattle weak Christians out of their salvation in Christ. What a dreadful thought that, like the characters of John Bunyan's *Pilgrim's Progress*, Mr. Fearing and Mr. Feeblemind, *you personally* might have an overly difficult time reading this treatise. You may certainly find yourself becoming a bit emotional through it. When the doctrine of spiritual examination is applied to any Christian, it can be a very trying journey to take. Examination is not necessarily a "fun spiritual time." When one goes to the Physician for some serious malady, they are put under examination to find out exactly what is going on; but such an examination is needful. The Psalmist, in grace, said, "Examine me, O LORD, and prove me; try my reins and my heart," (Psalm 26:2). The Apostle Paul exhorted in 1 Corinthians 11:28, "But let a man examine himself, and so let him eat of that bread, and drink of that cup," and in 2 Corinthians 13:5, "Examine yourselves, whether ye be in the faith; prove your own selves. Know ye not your own selves, how that Jesus Christ is in you, except ye be reprobates?" There is no doubt that verses such as these can be scary and frightening to the doubting believer who is not as assured as they could be in the saving power of

Christ. However, Mead says, that this treatise was not designed to "break the bruised reed, nor to quench the smoking flax." It is not meant to discourage the weakest believer, but *to awaken false professors.* He did not want to "sadden the hearts of any whom God would not have made sad," though, he says, "I know it is hard to expose the dangerous state and condition of a professing hypocrite, but that the weak Christian will think himself concerned in the discovery." His purpose in this is to help, and not hurt. Yet, no matter at what stage any spiritual inventory is taken, there is always a cleaning and ordering of the room. Take this to heart in considering the full storehouses of grace that Christ the Redeemer lavishes on his people, and be sure that you have a cup that is not only filled with good things from the throne of grace (*cf.* Psalm 23), but that such a cup is one which overflows with Christ's abundant grace.

Blessings in Christ,
C. Matthew McMahon, Ph.D.
From my study, February, 2019

Original Title Page

THE
Almost Christian
DISCOVERED;
OR, THE
FALSE PROFESSOR
TRIED and CAST.

Being the substance of seven
SERMONS

First preached at *Sepulchers, London*, 1661
And now at the importunity of Friends made Public.

BY *MATTHEW MEAD*

Luke 16:14, "And the Pharisees also, who were covetous, heard all these things: and they derided him."
Verse 15, "And he said unto them, Ye are they which justify yourselves before men; but God knoweth your hearts: for that which is highly esteemed among men is abomination in the sight of God."

LONDON,
Printed by *A.M.* for *Thomas Parkhurst*, at the *Bible* and the *Three Crowns* in *Cheapside*, and the *Bible* on *London Bridge*,
1671

To the Hearers

TO THE CONGREGATION AT ST. SEPULCHRE'S, THAT WERE THE AUDITORS OF THESE SERMONS, GRACE AND PEACE BE MULTIPLIED.

Beloved,

What was the meaning of that providence that called me to the occupation of my talent among you this summer, will be best read and understood by the effects of it on your own souls. The kindly increase of grace and holiness in heart and life, can only prove it to have been in mercy. Where this is not the fruit of the word, there it becomes a judgment. The word travels with *life or death, salvation or damnation*, and brings forth one or the other in every soul that hears it. I would not for a world (were it in my power to make the choice) that my labors, which were meant and designed for the promotion of your immortal souls to the glory of the other world, in a present pursuance of the things of your peace, should be found to have been a ministration of death and condemnation, in the great day of Jesus Christ. Yet, this, the Lord knows, is the too common effect of the most plain and powerful preaching of the Gospel. "The waters of the sanctuary" do not always heal where they come, for there are "miry and marshy places that shall be given to salt." The same word is elsewhere in Scripture rendered "barrenness;" He "turneth a fruitful land into barrenness," so that the judgment denounced on these miry and marshy places is, that the curse of barrenness shall rest on them, notwithstanding the "waters of the sanctuary overflow them."

It is said, with certainty, that the Gospel inflicts a death of its own, as well as the Law; or else how are those trees in Jude said to be "twice dead, and plucked up by the roots." Yes, that which in itself is the greatest mercy, through the interposition of men's lusts, and the efficacy of this cursed sin of unbelief, turns to the greatest judgment. This is like the richest and most generous wine makes the sharpest vinegar. Our Lord Christ himself, the choicest mercy with which the bowels of God could bless a perishing world, whose coming himself bearing witness, was on no less an errand than that of *eternal life* and blessedness to the lost and cursed sons of Adam. Yet, to how many was he a "stone of stumbling, and a rock of offence," yes, "a gin, and a snare;" and that to both the houses of Israel, the only professing people of God at that day in the world? And is he not a stone of stumbling in the ministry of the Gospel to many professors to this very day, on which they fall and are broken? When he says, "Blessed is he whosoever shall not be offended in me," he in this plainly supposes, that both in his person and doctrine generally men would be *offended in him*.

Not that this is the design of Christ and the Gospel, but it comes so to pass through the corruptions of the hearts of men, by which they make light of Christ, and stand out against that life and grace which the Lord Jesus by his blood so dearly purchased, and is by the preaching of the Gospel so freely tendered. The willful refusal of this will as surely double our damnation, as the acceptance of it will secure our eternal salvation.

O! consider, it is a thing of the most serious concern in the world, how we carry ourselves under the Gospel, and with what dispositions and affections of heart soul-seasons of grace are entertained. This should all be taken into the consideration to give it weight, that we are nearer to heaven or hell, to salvation or damnation, by every ordinance we sit under. Do not boast, therefore, of privileges you have enjoyed, with a neglect of the important duties by it that are actually required. Remember Capernaum's case and tremble. As many go to heaven by the very gates of hell, so more go to hell by the gates of heaven; in that the number of those that profess Christ is greater than the number of those that truly close with Christ.

Beloved, I know the preaching of the Gospel has proselyted many of you into a profession; but I fear that but few of you are brought by it to a true close with the Lord Christ for salvation. I beseech you to bear with my jealousy, for it is the fruit of a tender love for your precious souls. Most men are good Christians in the verdict of their own opinion; but you know the Law does not allow any man to be a witness in his own case, because their affection usually overreaches conscience, and self-love deceives truth for its own interest.

The heart of man is the greatest impostor and cheat in the world; God himself says it, "The heart is deceitful above all things," (Jer. 17:9). Some of the deceits of this you will find discovered in this *Treatise*, which shows you, that every grace has its counterfeit, and that the highest profession may be, where true conversion is not.

Its design is not to "break the bruised reed, nor to quench the smoking flax." Not to discourage the weakest believer, but to awaken formal professors. I would not sadden the hearts of any "whom God would not have made sad," though I know it is hard to expose the dangerous state and condition of a professing hypocrite, but that the weak Christian will think himself concerned in the discovery. And therefore, as I preached a sermon on sincerity among you, for the support and encouragement of such, so I purposed to have printed it with this. But who can be master of his own purposes? That is, as I am under such daily variety of providences, your kindly acceptance of this, will make me a debtor for that.

The dedication of this belongs to you on a double account; for as it had not been preached, but that love to your souls caused it, so it had much less been printed, but that your importunate desire procured it. And therefore, whatever entertainment it finds in the world, yet I hope I may expect you will welcome it, especially considering it was born under your roof, and therefore hopes to find favor in your eyes, and room in your hearts.

Accept it, I beseech you, as a public acknowledgment of the engagements which your great, and, I think I may say, unparalleled respects have laid me under, which I can no way compensate but by my prayers; and if you will take them for satisfaction, I promise to be your remembrancer at the throne of grace, while I am

MATTHEW MEAD

To the Reader

READER,

I know how customary it is for men to ascend the public stage with premised apologies for the weakness and unworthiness of their labors, which is an argument that their desires (either for the sake of others' profit, or their own credit, or both) are stretched beyond the bounds of their abilities. They covet to commend themselves to the world's censure, in a better dress than common infirmity will allow. For my own part, I may truly say with Gideon, "Behold, my thousand is the meanest," my talent is the smallest, "and I am the least in my Father's house." This appearance in public is not the fruit of my own choice, which would rather have been on some other subject, in which I stand in some sense indebted to the world, or else somewhat more digested, and possibly better fitted for common acceptation. But this is but to consult the interest of a man's own name, which, in matters of this concern, is no better than a "sowing to the flesh," and the harvest of such a seed-time will be "in corruption."

You have here one of the saddest considerations imaginable presented to you, and that is, "How far it is possible a man may go in a profession of religion, and yet, after all, fall short of salvation; how far he may run, and yet not so run as to obtain." This, I say, is sad, but not so sad as true; for our Lord Christ plainly attests it: "Strive to enter in at the strait gate; for many, I say unto you, will seek to enter in, and shall not be able," (Luke 13:24).

My design in this is, that the formal, sleepy professor may be awakened, and the close hypocrite discovered; but my fear is, that weak believers may be by this discouraged; for, as it is hard to show, how low a child of God may fall into sin, and yet have true grace, but that the sinner will be apt in this to presume; so it is as hard to show how high a hypocrite may rise in a profession, and yet have no grace, but that the believer will be apt on this to despond. To prevent this I have carefully endeavored, by showing, that though a man may go so far, and yet be but *almost a Christian*, yet a man may fall short of this, and be a true Christian notwithstanding. Do not judge, therefore, your state by any one character you find laid down of a false professor; but read the whole, and then make a judgment. I have cared, as not to "give children's bread to dogs," so not to use the dog's whip to scare the children; yet I could wish that this book might fall into the hands of such only whom it chiefly concerns, who "have a name to live, and yet are dead," being busy with the "form of godliness," but strangers to its "power." These are the proper subjects of this treatise. And may the Lord follow it with his blessing wherever it comes, that it may be an awakening word to all such, and especially to that generation of profligate professors with which this age abounds; who, if they keep to their church, bow the knee, talk over a few prayers, and at a good time receive the sacrament, think they do enough for heaven, and on this judge their condition safe, and their salvation sure; though there be a hell of sin in their hearts, "and the poison of asps is under their lips;" their minds being as yet carnal and unconverted, and their conversations filthy and unsanctified. If eternal life is of such an easy attainment, and to be had at such a cheap a rate, why did our Lord Christ tell us, "Strait is the gate and narrow is the way which leadeth unto life, and few there be that find it?" And why should the apostle perplex us with such a needless injunction, "to give diligence to make our calling and election sure?" Certainly, therefore, it is not an easy thing to be saved, as many make it; and you will see this plainly in the following discourse. I have been somewhat short in its application; and therefore, let me here be your remembrancer in five important duties:

First, "Take heed of resting in a *form of godliness*, as if duties, *ex opere operato*, could confer grace. A lifeless formality is advanced to a very high esteem in the world, as a "cab of dove's dung" was sold in the famine of Samaria at a very dear rate. Alas! the profession of godliness is but a sandy foundation to build the hope of an immortal soul on for eternity. Remember, the Lord Jesus Christ called him a foolish builder, "that founded his house upon the sand," and the sad event proved him so, "for it fell, and great was the fall of it." O! therefore lay thy foundation by faith on the *Rock* Christ Jesus; look to Christ through all, and rest on Christ in all.

Secondly, "Labor to see an excellency in the power of godliness," a beauty in the life of Christ, If the means of grace have a loveliness in them, surely grace itself has much more; for, "the goodness of the means lies in its suitableness and serviceableness to the end." The form of godliness has no goodness in it any further than it steads and becomes useful to the soul in the power and practice of godliness. The life of holiness is the only excellent life; it is the life of saints and angels in heaven; yes, it is the life of God in himself. As it is a great proof of the baseness and filthiness of sin, that sinners seek to cover it; so, it is a great proof of the excellency of godliness that so many pretend to it. The very hypocrite's fair profession pleads the cause of religion, although the hypocrite is then really worst, when he is seemingly best.

Thirdly, "Look upon things to come as the greatest realities;" for things that are not believed work no more upon the affections than if they had no being; and this is the grand reason why men in general suffer their affections to go after the world, setting the creature in the place of God in their hearts.

Most men judge of the reality of things by their visibility and proximity to sense; and, therefore, the choice of that wretched cardinal becomes their option, who would not leave his part in Paris for his part in Paradise. Sure, whatever his interest might be in the former, he had little enough in the latter. Well may covetousness be called idolatry, when it in this way chooses the world for its god.

O! consider, eternity is no dream; hell and the worm that never dies is no melancholy conceit. Heaven is no feigned Elysium; there is the greatest reality imaginable in these things; though they are spiritual, and out of the realm of physical sense now, yet they are real, and within the view of faith. "Look not therefore at the things which are seen, but look at the things which are not seen; for the things that are seen are temporal, but the things which are not seen are eternal," (2 Cor. 4:18).

Fourthly, "Set a high rate on your soul." What we lightly prize, we easily part with. Many men sell their souls at the rate of profane Esau's birth-right, for a morsel of bread;" no, "for that which," in the sense of the Holy Ghost, "is not bread." O! consider your soul is the most precious and invaluable jewel in the world; it is the most beautiful piece of God's workmanship in the whole creation; it is that which bears the image of God, and which was bought with the blood of the Son of God; and shall we not set a value upon it, and count it precious?

The apostle Peter speaks of three very precious things:

1. A precious Christ.
2. Precious Promises.
3. Precious Faith.

Now, the preciousness of all these lies in their usefulness to the soul. Christ is precious, as being the redeemer of precious souls. The *promises* are precious, as making over this precious Christ to precious souls. Faith is precious, as bringing a precious soul to close with a precious Christ, as he is held forth in the precious promises. O! take heed that you are not found overvaluing other things and undervaluing your soul. Shall your flesh, no, your heart, be loved, and shall your soul be slighted? Will you clothe and pamper your body, and yet take no care of your soul? This is, as if a man should feed his dog, and starve his child. "Meats for the belly, and the belly for meats; but God will destroy both it and them," (1 Cor. 6:13). O! do not let a tottering, perishing carcass have all your time and care, as if the life and salvation of your soul were not worth the while.

Lastly, "Meditate much on the strictness and suddenness of that judgment-day, through which you and

I must pass into an everlasting state; in which God, the impartial judge, will require an account at our hands of all our talents and entrustments." We must then account for time, how we have spent that; for estate, how we have employed that; for strength, how we have laid out that; for afflictions and mercies, how they have been improved; for the relations we stood in here, how they have been discharged; and for seasons and means of grace, how they have been husbanded. And look, how "we have sowed here, we shall reap hereafter."

    Reader, these are things that of all others deserve most of, and call loudest for, our utmost care and endeavors, though by the most least minded. To consider what a spirit of atheism is, we may judge the tree by the fruits, and the principle by the practice, the hearts of most men are filled with, who live, as if God were not to be served, nor Christ to be sought, nor lust to be mortified, nor self to be denied, nor the Scripture to be believed, nor the judgment-day to be minded, nor hell to be feared, nor heaven to be desired, nor the soul to be valued; but give up themselves to a worse than brutish sensuality, "to work all uncleanness with greediness," living without God in the world – this is a meditation fit enough to break our hearts, if at least we were of holy David's temper, who "beheld the transgressors, and was grieved," and had "rivers of waters running down his eyes, because men kept not God's Laws."

    The prevention and correction of this soul-destroying distemper, is not the least design of this *Treatise* now put into your hand. Though the chief virtue of this receipt lies in its sovereign use to assuage and cure the swelling tympany of hypocrisy, yet it may serve also,

To the Reader

with God's blessing, as a plaster for the plague-sore of profaneness, if timely applied by serious meditation, and carefully kept on by constant prayer.

Reader, expect nothing of curiosity or quaintness, for then I shall deceive you; but if you would have a touchstone for the trial of your state, possibly this may serve you. If you are either a stranger to a profession, or a hypocrite under a profession, then read and tremble, for you are the man here pointed at.[16]

But if the kingdom of God has come with power into your soul, if Christ is formed in you; if your heart is upright and sincere with God, then read and rejoice.

I fear I have transgressed the bounds of an epistle. The mighty God, whose prerogative it is to teach to profit, whether by the tongue or the pen, by speaking or writing, bless this *tract*, that it may be to thee as a cloud of rain to the dry ground, dropping fatness to your soul, that so your fleece being watered with the "dew of heaven," you may "grow in grace, and in the knowledge of our Lord and Savior Jesus Christ." In whom I am thy,

Friend and Servant,
MATTHEW MEAD

---

[16] *Mutato nomine de te Fabula narratur.* Horat.

Introduction

"Almost thou persuadest me to be a Christian," (Acts 26:28).

In this chapter you have the apostle Paul's apology and defensive plea which he makes for himself against those blind Jews which so maliciously prosecuted him before Agrippa, Festus, Bernice, and the council. In this plea he chiefly insists on three things.

1. The manner of his life before conversion.
2. The manner of his conversion.
3. The manner of his life after conversion.

How he lived before conversion, he tells you in verses 4-13. How God wrought on him to conversion, he tells you, verses 13-18. How he lived after conversion, he tells you, verses 19-23. Before conversion he was very pharisaical. The manner of his conversion was very wonderful. The fruit of his conversion was very remarkable.

Before conversion he persecuted the Gospel which others preached; after conversion he preached the Gospel which he had persecuted.

While he was a persecutor of the Gospel, the Jews loved him; but now that, by the grace of God, he became a preacher of the Gospel, now the Jews hate him, and sought to kill him.

He was once against Christ, and then many were for him; but now that he was for Christ, all were against him; his being an enemy to Jesus, made others his friends; but when he came to own Jesus, then they became his enemies. And this was the great charge they had against him, that of a great opposer he was become a great professor. Because God had changed him, therefore, this enraged them as if they would be the worse, because God had made him better. God had fashioned him by grace, and they seem to envy in him the grace of God. He preached no treason, nor sowed no sedition; only he preached repentance, and faith in Christ, and the resurrection, and for this he was "called in question."

This is the breviate and sum of Paul's defense and plea for himself, which, you find in the sequel of the chapter, had a different effect upon his judges.

Festus seems to censure him, verse 24. Agrippa seems to be convinced by him, verse 28. The whole bench seems to acquit him, verses 30-31. Festus thinks Paul was beside himself. Agrippa is *almost persuaded* to be such a one as himself.

Festus thinks he is mad because he did not understand the doctrine of Christ and the resurrection, "much learning hath made thee mad." Agrippa is so affected with his plea, that he is almost worked into his principle of being mad. Paul pleads so effectually for his religion, that Agrippa seems to be on a turning point to his profession. "Then Agrippa said to Paul, almost thou persuadest me to be a Christian."

"Almost." The words make some debate among the learned. I shall not trouble you with the various hints on them by Valla, Simplisius, Beza, Erasmus, and others. I take the words as we read them, and they show what an efficacy Paul's doctrine had on Agrippa's conscience. Though he would not be converted, yet he could not but be convinced his conscience was touched, though his heart was not renewed.

Observation. There is that in religion, which carries its own evidence along with it even to the consciences of ungodly men.

"Thou persuadest me." The word is from the Hebrew, and it signifies both *suadere* and *persuadere*, either to use arguments to prevail, or to prevail by the arguments used. Now it is to be taken in the latter sense here, to show the influence of Paul's argument on Agrippa, which had almost proselyted him to the profession of Christianity. "Almost thou persuadest me to be a Christian."

"A Christian." I hope I do not need to tell you what a Christian is, though I am persuaded many that are called Christians, do not know what a Christian is, or if they do, yet they do not know what it is to *be* a Christian. A Christian is a disciple of Jesus Christ, one that believes in, and follows Christ. As one that embraces the doctrine of Arminius is called an Arminian, and he that owns the doctrine and way of Luther, is called a Lutheran; so he that embraces, and owns, and follows the doctrine of Jesus Christ, he is called a Christian.

The word is taken more largely, and more strictly. It is more largely, and so all that profess that Christ came in the flesh, are called Christians, in opposition to heathens that do not know Christ; and to the poor blind Jews, that will not own Christ; and to the Islamic, that prefer Mahomet, above Christ. But now in Scripture, the word is of a more strict and narrow acceptance. It is used only to denominate the true disciples and followers of

Christ, "the disciples were first called Christians at Antioch; if any man suffer as a Christian, let him not be ashamed," (Acts 11:26); that is, as a member and disciple of Christ; and so in the text, "Almost thou persuadest me to be a Christian."

The word is used but in these three places, as I find, in all the New Testament, and in each of them it is used in the sense mentioned before.

The Italians make the name to be a name of reproach among them, and usually abuse the word Christian to signify a fool. But if, as the apostle says, "the preaching of Christ is to the world foolishness," (1 Cor. 1:21), then it is no wonder that the disciples of Christ are to the world fools. Yet it is true; in a sound sense, that so they are; for the whole of godliness is a mystery. A man must die, that would live; he must be empty, that would be full; he must be lost, that would be found; he must have nothing, that would have all things; he must be blind, that would have illumination; he must be condemned, that would have redemption; so he must be a fool that would be a Christian. "If any man among you seems to be wise, let him become a fool, that he may be wise," (1 Cor. 3:18). He is the true Christian that is the world's fool, but wise to salvation.

In this way, you have the sense and meaning of the words briefly explained. The text needs no division, and yet it is a pity the *almost* Christian should not be divided from the Christian. Though it is of little avail to divide them as they are linked in the text, unless I could divide them as they are united in your hearts; this would be a blessed division, if the *almost* might be taken from the

Christian that so you may not be only *propemodum*, but *admodum*; not only *almost*, but *altogether Christians*. This is God's work to effect it, but it is our duty to persuade to it; and O! that God would help me to manage this subject so, that you may say, in the conclusion, "Thou persuadest me, not almost, but *altogether* to be a Christian!"

The observation that I shall propound to handle is this DOCTRINE: There are very many in the world that are almost, and yet but almost Christians; many that are near heaven, and yet are never the nearer; many that are within a little of salvation, and yet shall never enjoy the least salvation; they are within sight of heaven, and yet shall never have a sight of God.

There are two sad expressions in Scripture, which I cannot but take notice of in this place. The one is concerning the truly righteous. The other is concerning the seemingly righteous.

It is said of the truly righteous, he shall "scarcely be saved," (1 Peter 4:18); and it is said of the seemingly righteous, he shall be almost saved, "You are not far from the kingdom of God," (Mark 12:34).

The righteous shall be saved with a *scarcely*, that is, through much difficulty; he shall go to heaven through many sad fears of hell. The hypocrite shall be saved with an *almost*, that is, he shall go to hell through many fair *hopes* of heaven.

There are two things which arise from here of very serious meditation. The one is, how often a believer may miscarry, how low he may fall, and yet have *true* grace. The other is, how far a hypocrite may go in the way to heaven, how high, he may attain, and yet have *no* grace.

Introduction

The saint may be cast down very near to hell, and yet shall never come there; and the hypocrite may be lifted up very near to heaven, and yet never come there. The saint may almost perish, and yet be saved eternally; the hypocrite may almost be saved, and yet perish finally. For the saint at worst is really a believer, and the hypocrite at best is really a sinner.

Before I handle the doctrine, I must premise three things, which are of great use for the establishing of weak believers, that they may not be shaken and discouraged by this doctrine.

First, there is nothing in the doctrine that should be a matter of stumbling or discouragement to weak Christians. The Gospel does not speak these things to wound believers, but to awaken sinners and formal professors.

As there are none more averse than weak believers, to apply the promises and comforts of the Gospel to themselves, for whom they are properly designed; so, there are none more ready than they to apply the threats and severest things of the word to themselves, for whom they were never intended. As the disciples, when Christ told them, "One of you shall betray me;" they that were innocent suspected themselves most, and therefore cry out, "Master, is it I?" So weak Christians, when they hear sinners reproved, or the hypocrite laid open, in the ministry of the word, they presently cry out, "Is it I?"

It is the hypocrite's fault to sit under the trials and discoveries of the word, and yet not to mind them. And it is the weak Christian's fault to draw sad conclusions of their own state from premises which nothing concerns them.

There is indeed great use of such doctrine as this is to all believers.

1. To make them look to their standing, upon what foundation they are, and to see that the foundation of their hope be well laid, that they build not upon the sand, but upon a rock.

2. It helps to raise our admiration of the distinguishing love of God, in bringing us into the way everlasting, when so many perish from the way, and in overpowering our souls into a true conversion, when so many take up with a graceless profession.

3. It incites to that excellent duty of heart-searching, so that we approve ourselves to God in sincerity.

4. It engages the soul in double diligence, that it may be found not only believing, but persevering in faith to the end.

These duties, and such as these, make this doctrine of use to all believers; but they ought not to make use of it as a stumbling-block in the way of their peace and comfort.

My design in preaching on this subject, is not to make sad the souls of those whom Christ will not have made sad; I would bring water not to "quench the flax that is smoking," but to put out that false fire that is of the sinner's own kindling, unless walking all his days by the light thereof, he shall at last "lie down in sorrow." My aim is to level the mountain of the sinner's confidence, not to weaken the hand of the believer's faith and dependence; to awaken and bring in secure formal sinners, not to discourage weak believers.

Secondly, I would premise this: though many may go far, very far in the way to heaven, and yet fall short, yet that soul that has the least true grace shall never fall short, for, "the righteous shall hold on his way," (Job 17:9).

Though some may do very much in a way of duty, as I shall show hereafter, and yet miscarry; yet that soul that does duty with the least sincerity, shall never miscarry; "for he saveth the upright in heart," (Psalm 7:10).

The least measure of true grace is as saving as the greatest; it saves as surely, though not so comfortably. The least grace gives a full interest in the blood of Christ, by which we are thoroughly purged; and it gives a full interest in the strength and power of Christ, by which we shall be certainly preserved.

Christ keeps faith in the soul, and faith keeps the soul in Christ; and so "we are kept by the power of God, through faith unto salvation," (1 Peter 1:5).

Thirdly, I would premise this; they that can hear such truths as this, without serious reflection and self-examination, I must suspect the goodness of their condition.

You will suspect that man to be next door to a bankrupt, that never casts up his accounts nor looks over his book; and I as verily think that man a hypocrite, that never searches nor deals with his own heart. He that goes on in a road of duties without any uneasiness or doubting of his state, I doubt no man's state more than his.

When we see a man sick, and yet not sensible, we conclude the tokens of death are on him. So, when sinners have no sense of their spiritual condition, it is plain that they are *dead in sin*; the tokens of eternal death are on them. These things being premised, which I desire you would carry along in your mind while we travel through this subject, I come to speak to the proposition more distinctly and closely.

DOCTRINE. That there are very many in the world that are almost, and yet but *almost* Christians.

I shall demonstrate the truth of the proposition, and then proceed to a more distinct prosecution.

I. I shall demonstrate the truth of the proposition; and I shall do it by scripture-evidence, which speaks plainly and fully to the case.

First, the young man in the Gospel is an eminent proof of this truth. There you read of one that came to Christ to learn of him the way to heaven, "Good Master, what good thing shall I do, that I may have eternal life?" Our Lord Christ tells him, "If thou wilt enter into life, keep the commandments:" and when Christ tells him which, he answers, "Lord, all these I have kept from my youth up; what lack I yet?" (Luke 18:21).

Now do but see how far this man went.

1. He obeyed; he did not only hear the commands of God, but he kept them; now the Scripture says, "Blessed is he that hears the word of God, and keeps it," (Luke 11:28).

2. He obeyed universally; not this or that command, but both this and that; he did not *halve* it with God, or pick and choose which were easiest to be done, and leave the rest; no, but he obeys *all*, "All these things have I kept."

3. He obeyed constantly; not in a fit of zeal only, but in a continual series of duty; his goodness was not, as

Introduction

Ephraim's, "like the morning dew that passes away;" no, "All these things have I kept from my youth up."

4. He professes desire to know and do more; to perfect that which was lacking of his obedience: and therefore, he goes to Christ to instruct him in his duty; "master, what lack I yet?" Now would you not think this a good man? Alas! how few go *this* far? And yet as far as he went, he went not far enough; "he was almost, and yet but *almost a Christian;*" for he was an unsound hypocrite; he forsakes Christ at last and cleaves to his lust. This then is a full proof of the truth of the doctrine.

Second, a second proof of it is that of the parable of the virgins in St. Matthew. See what a progress they make, how far they go in a profession of Christ.

1. They are called "virgins," (Matt. 25:1). Now this is a name given in the Scripture, both in the Old Testament and the New, to the saints of Christ, "The virgins love thee;" so in Revelation, the "one hundred forty and four thousand" that stood with the Lamb on Mount Zion, are called "virgins." They are called virgins, because they are not defiled with the "corruptions that are in the world through lust." Now these here seem to be of that sort, for they are called virgins.

2. They take their lamps; that is, they make a profession of Christ.

3. They had some kind of oil in their lamps. They had some convictions and some faith, though not the faith of God's elect, to keep their profession alive, to keep the lamp burning.

4. They went; their profession was not an idle profession; they did perform duties, frequented

ordinances, and did many things commanded: they made some progress; they went.

5. They went forth; they went and outwent, they left many behind them; this speaks about their separation from the world.

6. They went with the "wise virgins"; they joined themselves to those who had joined themselves to the Lord and were companions of them that were companions of Christ.

7. They go "forth to meet the bridegroom;" this speaks out their owning and seeking after Christ.

8. When they heard the cry of the bridegroom coming, "they arose and trimmed their lamps;" they profess Christ more highly, hoping now to go in with the bridegroom.

9. They sought for true grace. Now, do we not say, the desires of grace are grace? and they are, if they are true and timely, if they are sound and seasonable. Why, you see here a *desire of grace* in these virgins, "Give us of your oil?"

It was a desire of true grace, but it was not a true desire of grace; it was not true, because it was not timely; it was unsound, as being unseasonable; it was too late. Their folly was in not taking oil when they took their lamps; their time of seeking grace was when they came to Christ, it was too late to seek it when Christ came to them. They should have sought for that when they took up their profession. It was too late to seek it at the coming of the bridegroom. And therefore "they were shut out;" and though they cry for entrance, "Lord, Lord, open to us;" yet the Lord Christ tells them, "I know you not."

Introduction

You see how far these virgins go in a profession of Jesus Christ, and how long they continue in it, even until the bridegroom came; they go to the very door of heaven, and there, like the Sodomites, perish with their hands on the very threshold of glory. They were *almost* Christians, and yet but almost; almost saved, and yet perished.

You that are professors of the Gospel of Christ, stand and tremble. If they that have gone beyond us fall short of heaven, what shall become of us that fall short of them? If they that are virgins, that profess Christ, that have some faith in their profession, such as it is, that have some fruit in their faith, that outstrip others that seek Christ, that improve their profession, and suit themselves to their profession; no, that seek grace; if such as these be but almost Christians, Lord, what are we?

Third, if these two witnesses are not sufficient to prove the truth, and confirm the credit of the proposition, take a third; and that shall be from the Old Testament, in Isaiah 58:2. See what God says of that people; he gives them a very high character for a choice people, one would think, "They seek me daily; they delight to know my ways, as a nation that did righteousness, and forsook not the ordinance of their God; they ask of me the ordinances of justice; they take delight in approaching to God."

See how far these went; if God had not said they were rotten and unsound, we should have taken them for the "he-goats before the flock," and ranked them among the worthies. I pray that you would observe the *following:*

1. They seek God. Now this is the proper character of a true saint, to seek God. True saints are called, "seekers of God." "This is the generation of them that seek him, that

seek thy face, O Jacob" or, "O God of Jacob." So, here is a generation of them that seek God, and are *not* these the saints of God? No, *further:*

2. They seek him daily. Here is diligence backed with continuance, day by day; that is, every day, from day to day. They did not seek him by fits and starts, nor in a time of trouble and affliction only, as many do. "Lord, in trouble have they visited thee; they poured out a prayer when thy chastening was upon them." Many when, God visits them, then they visit him, but not until then; when God pours out his afflictions, then they pour out their supplications. This is seamen's devotion; when the storms have brought them to "their wits' end, then they cry to the Lord in their trouble." Many never cry to God, until they are at their wits' end; they never come to God for help, so long as they can help themselves. But now these here, whom God speaks of, these who are more zealous in their devotion; the others make a virtue of necessity, but these seem to make conscience of duty; for, God says, "they seek me daily." Surely this is, one would think, a note of sincerity. Job says of the hypocrite, "Will he always call upon God?" Surely not; but now this people call on God always, "they seek him daily;" certainly these cannot be hypocrites.

3. God says, "They delight to know my ways." Surely this frees them from the suspicion of hypocrisy; for, they do not say to God, "Depart from us; we desire not the knowledge of thy ways."

4. They are "as a nation that did righteousness." Not only as a nation that spoke righteousness, or knew righteousness, or professed righteousness, but as a nation

that *did* righteousness, that practiced nothing but what was just and right. They appeared, to the judgment of the world, as good as the best.

5. They did not forsake the ordinances of their God. They seem true to their principles, constant to their profession, better than many among us, that cast off duties, and forsake the ordinances of God: but these hold out in their profession; "they forsook not the ordinances of God."

6. "They ask of me," God says, "the ordinances of justice." They will not make their own will the rule of right and wrong, but the Law and will of God: and therefore, in all their dealings with men, they desire to be guided and counseled by God, "They ask of me the ordinances of justice."

7. They take delight in approaching to God. Surely this cannot be the guise of a hypocrite. "Will he delight himself in the Almighty?" Job says; no, he will not. Though God is the chief delight of man, (having everything in him to render him lovely, as was said of Titus Vespasian,) yet the hypocrites will not delight in God. Until the affections are made spiritual, there is no affection to things that are spiritual. God is a spiritual good, and therefore hypocrites cannot delight in God. But these are a people that delight in approaching to God.

8. They were a people that were much in fasting: "Wherefore have we fasted," say they, "and thou seest not?" Now this is a duty that does not suppose and require truth of grace only in the heart, but strength of grace.

"No man," our Lord Christ says, "puts new wine into old bottles, lest the bottles break and the wine run out." New wine is strong, and old bottles weak; and the strong wine breaks the weak vessel. This is a reason Christ gives, why his disciples, who were newly converted, and but weak as yet, were not exercised with this austere discipline. But this people here mentioned were a people that fasted often, afflicted their souls much, wore themselves out by frequent practices of humiliation. Surely therefore this was "new wine in new bottles;" this must necessarily be a people strong in grace; there seems to be grace not only in truth, but also in growth. And yet, for all this, they were no better than *a generation of hypocrites*; they made a goodly progress, and went far, but yet they went not far enough; they were cast off by God after all.

I hope by this time the truth of the point is sufficiently admitted and confirmed; "that a man may be, yes, very many are, *almost*, and yet no more than but *almost Christians.*"

Now for the more distinct prosecution of the point, 1. I shall show you, step by step, how far he may go, to what attainments he may reach, how specious and singular a progress he may make in religion, and yet be but *almost a Christian* when all is done.

2. I will show where it is that many men go so far as that they are almost Christians.

3. Why they are but almost Christians when they have gone so far.

4. What the reason is, why men that go so far as to be almost Christians yet go no farther than to be almost Christians.

Question 1

How far may a man go in the way to heaven, and yet be but *almost a Christian*?

Answer. This I will show you in twenty steps.

I. A man may have much knowledge, much light; he may know much of God and his will, much of Christ and his ways, and yet be but *almost a Christian*.

For though there can be no grace without knowledge, yet there may be much knowledge where there is no grace; illumination often goes before, when conversion never follows after. The subject of knowledge is the understanding; the subject of holiness is the will. Now a man may have his understanding enlightened, and yet his will may not be at all sanctified. He may have an understanding to know God, and yet need a will to obey God. The apostle tells us of some, that, "when they knew God, they glorified him not as God."

To make a man altogether a Christian, there must be light in the head, and beat in the heart; knowledge in the understanding, and zeal in the affections. Some have zeal and no knowledge; that is, blind devotion; some have knowledge and no zeal; that is, fruitless speculation: but where knowledge is joined with zeal, that makes a true Christian.

OBJECTION. But is it not said, this is life eternal, "to know thee, the only true God, and Jesus Christ whom thou hast sent?" (John 17:3).

Answer. It is not every knowledge of God and Christ, that interests the soul in life eternal. For why then do the devils perish? They have more knowledge of God than all the men in the world; for though, by their fall, they lost their holiness, yet they did not lose their knowledge. They are called *daimones*, from their knowledge, and yet they are *diaboloi*, from their malice, devils still.

Knowledge may fill the head, but it will never better the heart, if there is not something else. The Pharisees had much knowledge, "Behold, you are called a Jew, and restest in the Law, and makest thy boast of God, and knowest his will," *etc.* (Rom. 2:17), and yet they were a generation of hypocrites. Alas! how many have gone loaded with knowledge to hell!

Though it is true, that it is life eternal to know God and Jesus Christ; yet it is as true, that many do know God and Jesus Christ, that shall never see life eternal. There is, you must know, a twofold knowledge; the one is common, but not saving; the other is not common, but saving. Common knowledge is that which floats in the head but does not influence the heart. This knowledge, reprobates may have, "Balaam saw Christ from the top of the rocks, and from the hills."

Naturalists say, that there is a pearl in the toad's head, and yet her belly is full of poison. The French have a berry which they call *uve de spine*, the grape of a thorn. The common knowledge of Christ is the pearl in the toad's head, and the grape that grows upon thorns; it may be found in men unsanctified.

And then there is a saving knowledge of God and Christ, which includes the assent of the mind, and the consent of the will; this is a knowledge that implies faith, "By his knowledge shall my righteous servant justify many." And this is that knowledge which leads to life eternal. Now whatever that measure of knowledge is, which a man may have of God, and of Jesus Christ, yet if it is not this saving knowledge; knowledge joined with affection and application; he is but *almost a Christian*.

He only knows God aright, who knows how to obey him, and obeys according to his knowledge of him: "A good understanding have all they that do his commandments." All knowledge without this makes a man but like Nebuchadnezzar's image, with "a head of gold, and feet of clay."

Some know, but to know.
Some know, to be known.
Some know, to practice what they know.
Now, to know, but to know; that is curiosity.
To know, to be known; that is vain glory.
But to know, to practice what we know; that is Gospel duty. This makes a man a complete Christian; the other, without this, makes a man almost, and yet but *almost a Christian*.

II. A man may have great and eminent gifts, yes, spiritual gifts, and yet be but *almost a Christian*.

The gift of prayer is a spiritual gift. Now this a man may have, and yet be but *almost a Christian*. For the gift of prayer is one thing; the grace of prayer is another. The gift of preaching and prophesying is a spiritual gift; now this a man may have, and yet be but *almost a Christian*. Judas was a great preacher; so were they that came to Christ, and said, "Lord, Lord, we have prophesied in thy name, and in thy name have cast out devils," *etc.*

You must know that it is not gifts, but grace, which makes a Christian: *For,*

1. Gifts are from a common work of the Spirit. Now a man may partake of all the common gifts of the Spirit, and yet be a reprobate; for therefore they are called *common*, because they are indifferently dispensed by the Spirit to good and bad; to them that are believers, and to them that are not.

They that have grace have gifts; and they that have no grace, may have the same gifts; for the Spirit works in both; no, in this sense he that has no grace, may be under a greater work of the Spirit (*quod hoc*) as to this thing, than he who has most grace. A graceless professor may have greater gifts than the most holy believer. He may out-pray, and out-preach, and out-do them; but they in sincerity and integrity *out-go him.*

2. Gifts are for the use and good of others, they are given in *ordinem alium*, as the schoolmen speak, for the profiting and edifying of others. So, the apostle says, "they are given to profit withal," (1 Cor. 12:7). Now a man may edify another by his gifts, and yet be unedified himself; he may be profitable to another, and yet unprofitable to himself.

The raven was an unclean bird. God makes use of her to feed Elijah; though she was not good meat, yet it was good meat she brought. A lame man may with his crutch point to the right way, and yet not be able to walk in it himself. A crooked tailor may make a suit to fit a straight body, though it does not fit him that made it, because of

Question 1

his crookedness. The church (Christ's garden enclosed) may be watered through a wooden gutter; the sun may give light through a dusky window; and the field may be well sowed with a dirty hand.

The efficacy of the word does not depend on the authority of him that speaks it, but on the authority of God that blesses it. So that another may be converted by my preaching, and yet I may be cast away notwithstanding. Balaam makes a clear and rare prophecy of Christ, and yet he has no benefit by Christ: "There shall come a star out of Jacob, and a sceptre shall rise out of Israel;" but yet Balaam shall have no benefit by it, "I shall see him, but not now; I shall behold him, but not nigh," (Num. 24:17).

God may use a man's gifts to bring another to Christ, when he himself, whose gifts God uses, may be a stranger to Christ; one man may confirm another in the faith, and yet himself may be a stranger to the faith. Pendleton strengthens and confirms Sanders, in Queen Mary's days, to stand in the truth he had preached, and to seal it with his blood, and yet afterwards plays the apostate himself.

Scultetus tells us of one Johannes Speiserus, a famous preacher of Augsburg in Germany, in the year 1523, who preached the Gospel so powerfully that diverse common harlots were converted and became good Christians. Yet, himself afterwards turned papist and came to a miserable end. In this way, the candle may burn bright to light others in their work, and yet afterwards go out in a stink.

3. It is beyond the power of the greatest gifts to change the heart; a man may preach like an apostle, pray

like an angel, and yet may have the heart of a devil. It is only grace that can change the heart; the greatest gifts cannot change it, but the least grace can. Gifts may make a man a scholar, but grace makes a man a believer. Now if gifts cannot change the heart, then a man may have the greatest gifts, and yet be but *almost a Christian*.

4. Many have gone laden with gifts to hell; no doubt Judas had great gifts, for he was a preacher of the Gospel; and our Lord Jesus Christ would not set him to work, and not fit him for the work; yet "Judas is gone to his own place," (Acts 1:25). The Scribes and Pharisees were men of great gifts, and yet, "where is the wise? where is the scribe?" (1 Cor. 1:20).

"The preaching of the cross is to them that perish foolishness," (1 Cor. 1:18). Them that perish, who are they? These are the wise and the learned, both among Jews and Greeks; these are called "them that perish." A great bishop said, when he saw a poor shepherd weeping over a toad, "The poor illiterate world attains to heaven, while we with all our learning fall into hell."

There are three things that must be done for us, if we would ever avoid perishing.

We must be thoroughly convinced of sin.

We must be really united to Christ.

We must be instated in the covenant of grace.

Now, the greatest gifts cannot keep us in any of these.

They cannot work thorough convictions.

They cannot affect our union.

They cannot bring us into covenant-relation.

And consequently, they cannot preserve us from eternally perishing; and if so, then a man may have the greatest gifts, and yet be but *almost a Christian*.

5. Gifts may decay and perish. They do not lie beyond the reach of corruption; indeed, grace shall never perish, but gifts will. Grace is incorruptible, though gifts are not; grace is "a spring, whose waters fail not," (Isa. 58:11), but the streams of gifts may be dried up. If grace is corruptible in its own nature, as being but a creature, yet it is incorruptible in regard of its conserver, as being the new creature; he that created it in us, will conserve it in us; he that began it will also finish it.

Gifts have their root in nature, but grace has its roots in Christ; and therefore, though gifts may die and wither, yet grace shall abide forever. Now if gifts are perishing, then, though he that has the least grace is a Christian, he that has the greatest gifts may be but *almost a Christian*.

OBJECTION. But does not the apostle bid us "covet earnestly the best gifts?" Why must we covet them, and covet them earnestly, if they do not avail to salvation?

Answer. Gifts are good, though they are not the best good; they are excellent, but there is something more excellent, so it follows in the same verse, "Yet I show unto you a more excellent way," and that is the way of grace. One dram of grace is more worth than a talent of gifts. Gifts may make us rich towards men, but it is grace that makes us "rich towards God." Our gifts profit others, but grace profits ourselves; that by this another might profit of my work towards them as a gift, but that by which I am profited myself is better in grace.

Now because gifts are good, therefore, we ought to covet them; but because they are not the best good, therefore we ought not to *rest* in them. We must covet gifts for the good of others, that they may be edified; and we must covet grace for the good of our own souls, that they may be saved; for whosoever is bettered by our gifts, yet we shall miscarry without grace.

III. A man may have a high profession of religion, be much in external duties of godliness, and yet be but *almost a Christian*.

Mark what our Lord tells them, "Not everyone that saith unto me, Lord, Lord, shall enter into the kingdom of heaven," (Matthew 7:21), that is, not every one that makes a profession of Christ, shall therefore be owned as a true disciple of Christ. "All are not Israel that are of Israel," (Romans 9:6), nor are all Christians that make a profession of religion.

What a godly profession had Judas! He followed Christ, left all for Christ, he preached the Gospel of Christ, he cast out devils in the name of Christ, he ate and drank at the table of Christ; and yet Judas was a hypocrite.

Most professors are like lilies, fair in show, but foul in scent; or like pepper, hot in the mouth, but cold in the stomach. The finest lace may be on the coarsest cloth.

It is a great deceit to measure the substance of our religion by the bulk of our profession, and to judge of the strength of our graces by the length of our duties. The Scriptures speak of some who having "a form of godliness, yet deny the power thereof," (2 Tim. 3:5). *Deny the power,* that is, they do not live in the practice of those graces to which they pretend in their duties. He that pretends to be godly by a specious profession, and yet does not practice godliness by a holy conversation, he has a form, but denies the power. Grotius compares such to the ostrich, which has great wings, but yet does not fly. Many have the wings of a fair profession, but they do not yet use them to mount upward in spiritual affections, and a heavenly conversation.

But to clear the truth of this, that a man may make a high profession of religion, and yet be but *almost a Christian*, take a fourfold evidence.

1. If a man may profess religion, and yet never have his heart changed, nor his state bettered, then he may be a great professor, and yet be but *almost a Christian*. But a man may profess religion, and yet never have his heart changed, nor his state renewed. He may be a constant hearer of the word, and yet be a sinner still; he may come often to the Lord's table, and yet go away a sinner as he came; we must not think that duties can confer grace.

Many a soul has been converted by Christ in an ordinance, but never was any soul converted by an ordinance without Christ. And does Christ convert all that sit under the ordinances? Surely not; for to some, "the word is a savor of death unto death," (2 Cor. 2:16). And if so, then it is plain, that a man may profess religion, and yet be but *almost a Christian*.

2. A man may profess religion and live in a form of godliness in hypocrisy. Hear ye this, O house of Jacob, which are called by the name of Israel, and are come forth out of the waters of Judah; which swear by the name of the Lord, and make mention of the God of Israel, but not in

truth, nor in righteousness." What do you think of these? "They make mention of the name of the Lord, there is their profession but not in truth; nor in righteousness," there is their dissimulation: and indeed there could be no hypocrisy in a religious sense, were it not for a profession of religion; for he that is wicked and carnal, and vile inwardly, and appears to be so outwardly, he is no hypocrite, but is what he appears, and appears what he is. But he that is one thing really, and another thing seemingly, is carnal and unholy, and yet seems to be good and holy, he is a hypocrite.

In this way, the Casuists define hypocrisy to be a counterfeiting of holiness; and this fits exactly with the Greek word, which is, *to counterfeit.*

And to this purpose, the Hebrews have two words for hypocrites; *panim*, which signifies faces; and *chanepim*, which signifies counterfeits; from *chanaph*, to dissemble. So, he is a hypocrite that dissembles religion, and wears the face of holiness, and yet is without the grace of holiness. He appears to be in semblance, what he is not in substance; he wears a form of godliness without, only as a cover of a profane heart within. He has a profession that he may not be thought wicked; but it is but a profession, and therefore he is wicked. He is the religious hypocrite; religious, because he pretends to it; and yet a hypocrite, because he does *but pretend to it.* He is like many men in the sickness of consumption, that have fresh looks, and yet rotten lungs; or like an apple that has a fair skin, but a rotten core. Many appear righteous, who are, only righteous in appearance. And if so, then a man may profess religion, and yet be but *almost a Christian.*

3. Custom and fashion may make a man a professor; as you have many that wear this or that garb, not because it keeps them warmer, or has any excellency in it more than another, but merely for fashion.

Many must have powdered hair, spotted faces, feathers in their caps, *etc.*, for no other end, but because they would be fools in fashion. So, many profess Christianity not because the means of grace warm the heart, or that they see any excellencies in the ways of God above the world, but, merely to follow the fashion! I wish I might not say, it has been true of our days, because religion has been uppermost, therefore many have professed; it has been the gaining trade, and then most will be of that trade.

Religion in credit makes many professors, but few proselytes; but when religion suffers, then its confessors are no more than its converts; for custom makes the former, but conscience the latter. He that is a professor of religion merely for custom-sake, when it prospers, will never be a martyr for Christ's sake, when religion suffers. He that owns the truth, to live on that, will disown it, when it comes to live on him and presses him to act in godliness.

They say, that when a house is decaying or falling, all the rats and mice will forsake it; while the house is firm, and they may shelter in the roof, they will stay, but no longer; unless, in the decay, the fall should be on them, and they that lived at top should die at the bottom. My brethren, may I not say, we have many that are the vermin, the rats and mice of religion, that would live under its roof, while they might have shelter in it; but when it suffers, forsake it, unless it should fall, and the fall should be upon them? I am persuaded this is not the least reason why God has brought the wheel on the profession of religion; namely to rid it of the vermin. He shakes the foundations of the house, that these rats and mice may quit the roof; not to overturn it, but to rid them of it. This is as when the husbandman fans the wheat, that he may get rid of the chaff. The *calming* days of the Gospel provoke hypocrisy, but the sufferings for religion prove sincerity.

Now, then, if custom and fashion make many men professors, then a man may profess religion, and yet be but *almost a Christian*.

4. If many may perish under a profession of godliness, then a man may profess religion and yet be but *almost a Christian*.

Now, the Scripture is clear, that a man may perish under the highest profession of religion. Christ cursed the fig-tree that had leaves and no fruit. It is said, that "the children of the kingdom shall be cast out into outer darkness." Who were these, but they that were then the only people of God in the world by profession, that had made a "covenant with him by sacrifice"; and yet these were cast out.

In St. Matthew, you read of some that came and made boast of their profession to Christ, hoping that might save them. "Lord," say they, "have we not prophesied in thy name, cast out devils in thy name, done many wonderful works in thy name?" Now what does our Lord Christ say to this? "Then I will profess unto them, I never knew you; depart from me," (Matthew 25:41).

Mark, here are they that prophesy in his name, and yet perish in his wrath; in his name cast out devils, and

Question 1

then are cast out themselves; in his name do many wonderful works, and yet perish for wicked workers. The profession of religion will no more keep a man from perishing, than calling a ship the *Safe-guard*, or the *Good-speed*, will keep her from drowning. As many go to heaven with the fear of hell in their hearts, so many go to hell with the name of Christ in their mouths. Now then, if many may perish under a profession of godliness, then may a man be a high professor of religion, and yet be but *almost a Christian*.

OBJECTION. But is it not said by the Lord Christ himself, "He that confesses me before men, him will I confess before my Father in heaven?" Now, for Christ to say he will confess us before the Father, is equivalent to a promise of eternal life, for if Jesus Christ confess us, God the Father will never disown us.

True, they that confess Christ, shall be confessed by him; and it is as true, that this confession is equivalent to a promise of salvation. But now you must know, that professing Christ, is not confessing him: for to profess Christ is one thing; to confess Christ is another. Confession is a living testimony for Christ, in a time when religion suffers; profession may be only a lifeless formality, in a time when religion prospers. To confess Christ, is to choose his ways, and own them. To profess Christ, is to plead for his ways, and yet live beside them. Profession may be from a feigned love to the ways of Christ; but confession is from a rooted love to the person of Christ. To profess Christ, is to own him when none deny him; to confess Christ, is to plead for him, and suffer for him, when others oppose him. Hypocrites may be professors; but the martyrs are the true confessors. Profession is a swimming down the stream. Confession is a swimming against the stream. Now many may swim with the stream, like the dead fish, that cannot swim against the stream, with the living fish. Many may profess Christ, that cannot confess Christ; and so, notwithstanding their profession, yet are but almost Christians.

IV. To come yet nearer; a man may go far in opposing his sin, and yet be but *almost a Christian*.

How far a man may go in this work, I shall show you in seven gradual instances.

First, A man may be convinced of sin, and yet be but *almost a Christian. For,*

1. Conviction may be rational, as well as spiritual; it may be from a natural conscience enlightened by the word, without the effectual work of the Spirit, applying sin to the heart.

2. Convictions may be worn out; they many times go off, and do not end in a sound conversion. The Church says in Isaiah 26:18, "We have been with child, we have been in pain, we have brought forth wind." This is the complaint of the church, in reference to the unprofitableness of their afflictions; and it may be the complaint in most, in reference to the unprofitableness of their convictions.

3. Many take *conviction* of sin, to be *conversion* from sin; and to sit down and rest in their convictions. That is a sad complaint God makes of Ephraim in Hosea 13:13, "Ephraim is an unwise son; for he should not stay long in the place of the breaking forth of children." Now

then, if convictions may be only from natural conscience; if they may be worn out, or may be mistaken, and rested in for conversion, then a man may have convictions, and be but *almost a Christian.*

Secondly, a man may mourn for sin, and yet be but *almost a Christian.* So did Saul; so did Esau, for the loss of his birthright, which was his sin, and therefore he is called, by the Spirit of God, "profane Esau;" yet, "he sought it again carefully with tears," (Heb. 12:16).

OBJECTION. But does not Christ pronounce them blessed that mourn? "Blessed are they that mourn." Sure then, if a man mourns for sin, he is in a good condition: you see, Nazianzen says, that salvation is joined with sorrow.

Solution. I answer, it is true, that they who mourn for sin, in the sense Christ there speaks of, are blessed; but all mourning for sin, does not therefore render us blessed.

1. True mourning for sin must flow from spiritual convictions of the evil, and vileness, and damnable nature of sin. Now, all that mourn for sin, do not do it from a thorough work of spiritual conviction on the soul. They do not have a right sense of the evil and vileness of sin.

2. True mourning for sin, is more for the evil that is in sin, than the evil that comes by sin; more because it dishonors God, and wounds Christ, and grieves the Spirit, and makes the soul unlike God, than because it damns the soul. Now there are many that mourn for sin, not so much for the evil that is in it, as for the evil that it brings with it. There is mourning for sin in hell. You read of "weeping and wailing" there. The damned are weeping and mourning to eternity; there is all sorrow, and no comfort. As in heaven there is peace without trouble, joy without mourning, so

in hell there is trouble without peace, mourning without joy, weeping and wailing incessantly; but it is for the evil they feel by sin, and not for the evil that is in sin; so that a man may mourn for sin, and yet be but *almost a Christian*. It may grieve him to think of perishing for sin, when it does not grieve him that he is defiled and polluted by sin.

Thirdly, a man may make large confession of sin, to God, to others, and yet be but *almost a Christian*.

How ingenuously does Saul confess his sin to David? "I have sinned," he says, "you are more righteous than I! Behold, I have played the fool, and have erred exceedingly," (1 Sam. 26:21). So, Judas makes a full confession, "I have sinned in betraying innocent blood," (Matthew 27:4). Yet Saul and Judas were both rejected of God; so that a man may confess sin, and yet be but *almost a Christian*.

OBJECTION. But is not a confession of sin a character of a child of God? Does not the apostle say, "If we confess our sins, God is just and faithful to forgive them;" no man was ever kept out of heaven for his confessed badness, though many are kept out of heaven for their supposed goodness.

Judah, in Hebrew, signifies *confession*; now Judah got the kingdom from Reuben; confession of sin is the way to the kingdom of heaven.

There are some that confess sin and are saved; there are others that confess sin and perish.

1. Many confess sin merely out of custom, and not out of conscience; you shall have many that will never pray, but they will make a long confession of sin, and yet never feel the weight or burden of it on their consciences.

2. Many will confess lesser sins, and yet conceal greater; like the patient in Plutarch that complained to his physician of his finger when his liver was rotten.

3. Many will confess sin in general, or confess themselves sinners, and yet see little, and say less of their particular sins. An implicit confession, as one says, is almost as bad as an implicit faith.

Where confession is right, it will be distinct, especially of those sins that were our chief sins. So, David confesses his blood-guiltiness and adultery. Paul confesses his blasphemy, persecution, and injury against the saints. It is bad to hear men confess they are great sinners, and yet cannot confess their sins. Though the least sin is too *bad* to be committed, yet there is no sin too bad to be confessed.

4. Many will confess sin, but it is only under extremity, that is, not free and voluntary. Pharaoh confesses his sin, but it was when judgment compelled him. "I have sinned against the Lord," he says; but it was when he had had eight plagues upon him, (Exod. 10:16).

5. Many do by their sins as mariners do by their goods, cast them out in a storm, wishing for them again in a calm. Confession should come like water out of a spring, which runs freely; not like water out of a still, which is forced by fire.

6. Many confess their sins, but with no intent to forsake sin; they confess the sins they have committed, but do not leave the sins they have confessed.

Many men use their confession as Lewis XI of France did his crucifix; he would swear an oath, and then kiss it; and swear again, and then kiss it again. So many sin, and then confess they do not do well, but yet *never strive to do better.*

Mr. Torsel tells a story of a minister he knew, that would be often drunk, and when he came into the pulpit, would confess it very lamentingly; and yet no sooner was he out of the pulpit, but he would be drunk again; and this would he do as constantly as men follow their trades.

Now then, if a man may confess sin merely out of custom, if he may confess lesser sins, and yet conceal greater, if he may confess sin only in the general, or only under extremity, or if he may confess sin without any intent to forsake sin, then surely a man may confess sin, and yet be but *almost a Christian.*

Fourthly, a man may forsake sin, and yet be but *almost a Christian;* he may leave his lust, and his wicked ways, which he sometimes lived in, and in the judgment of the world become a new man, and yet not be a new creature. Simon Magus, when he hears Philip preaching concerning the kingdom of God, leaves his sorcery and witchcraft, *and believes.*

OBJECTION. But you will say, this seems contrary to Scripture; for that says, "He that confesseth and forsaketh sin, shall have mercy;" but I confess sin, yes, not only so, but also, I forsake sin; surely, therefore, this mercy is my portion, it belongs to me.

Answer. It is true, that where a soul forsakes sin *from a right principle,* after a right manner, to a right end, where he forsakes sin as sin, as being contrary to God, and the purity of his nature, this declares that soul to be right with God, and the promise shall be made good to it, "He shall find mercy," (2 Tim. 1:18).

But now consider deeply in your mind, there is a forsaking sin that is not right, but unsound.

1. Open sins may be deserted, and yet secret sins may be retained; now this is not a right forsaking; such a soul shall never find mercy. A man may be cured of a wound in his flesh, and yet may die of a disease in his bowels.

2. A man may forsake sin, but not as sin; for he that forsakes sin as sin, forsakes all sin. It is impossible for a man to forsake sin as sin, unless he forsakes all that he knows to be sin.

3. A man may let one sin go to hold another the faster; as a man that goes to sea, would willingly save all his goods; but if the storm arises that he cannot, then he throws some overboard to lighten the vessel, and save the rest. So they did in Acts 26:38. So the sinner chooses to keep all his sins; but if a storm arises in his conscience, he will heave *one* lust overboard to save the life of another.

4. A man may let all sin go, and yet be a sinner still; for there is the root of all sin in the heart, though the fruit is not seen in the life; the tree lives, though the boughs be lopped off. As a man is a sinner, before ever he acts sin, so (until grace renews him) he is a sinner, though he leaves sin; for there is original sin in him enough to damn and destroy him.

5. Sin may be left, and yet be loved; a man may forsake the life of sin, and yet retain the love of sin. Now, though leaving sin makes him *almost a Christian*, yet loving sin shows he is *but almost a Christian*. It is a less evil to do sin, and not love it, than to love sin and not do it; for to do sin may argue only weakness of grace, but *to love*

sin argues strength of lust. "What I hate, that I do." Sin is bad in any part of man, but sin in the affection is worse than sin in the conversation; for sin in the conversation may be only from infirmity, but sin in the affection is the fruit of choice and unregeneracy.

6. All sin may be chained, and yet the heart not changed; and so the nature of the sinner is the same as ever. A dog chained up, is still a dog, as much as if he was let loose to devour.

There may be a cessation of arms between enemies, and yet the quarrel may remain on foot still. There may be a truce made, where there is no peace made.

A sinner may lay the weapons of sin out of his hand, and yet the enmity against God still remain in his heart. There may be a truce; he may not sin against him; but there can be no peace until he be united to him.

Restraining grace holds something in the sinner, but it is renewing grace that changes his nature. Now, many in the world are restrained in by God's power from being open sinners, that are not renewed by grace, and made true believers.

Now then, if a man may forsake open sins, and retain secret sins; if he may forsake sin, but not as sin; if he may let one sin go, to hold another the faster; if a man may let all sin go, and yet be a sinner still; if sin may be left, and yet be loved. Finally, if all sin may be chained, and yet the heart not changed, then a man may forsake sin, and yet be but *almost a Christian.*

V. A man may hate sin, and yet be *almost a Christian.*

Question 1

Absalom hated Amnon's uncleanness with his sister Tamar. Yes, his hatred was so great, that he killed him for it; and yet Absalom was a wicked man.

OBJECTION. But the Scripture makes it a sign of a gracious heart, to hate sin; yes, though a man through infirmities, fall into sin, yet if he hates it, this is a proof of grace. Paul proves the sincerity of his heart, and the truth of his grace, by this hatred of sin, though he committed it: "What I hate, that I do." No, what is grace but a conformity of the soul to God; to love as God loves, to hate as God hates? Now God hates sin. It is one part of his holiness to hate all sin. And if I hate sin, then am I conformed to God. And if I am conformed to God, then am I altogether a Christian.

Answer. It is true, that there is a hatred of sin, which is a sign of grace, and which flows from a principle of grace, and is grace. As for *instance:*

To hate sin as an offence to God, a wrong to his majesty. To hate sin as a breach of his command, and so this is a wicked attempt at controlling of God's will, which is the only rule of goodness. To hate sin as being a disingenuous transgression of that Law of love established in the blood and death of Christ, and so, in a degree, a crucifying of Christ afresh. To hate sin, as being a grieving and quenching of the Spirit of God, as all sin in its nature is. In this way, to hate sin, is grace; and so every true Christian hates sin.

But, though every man that has grace hates sin, yet every man that hates sin does not have grace. For, a man may hate sin from other principles, not as it is a wrong to God, or a wounding Christ, or a grieving the Spirit; for then he would hate *all* sin; for there is no sin but has this in the nature of it. *But:*

1. A man may hate sin for the shame that attends it, more than for the evil that is in it. There are some sinners, "who declare their sin as Sodom, and hide it not," (Isa. 3:9). They are set down in the seat of the scornful; "they glory in their shame," (Phil. 3:19). But there are now others who are ashamed of sin, and therefore hate it, not for the sin's sake, but for the shame's sake. This made Absalom hate Amnon's uncleanness, because it brought shame on him and his sister.

2. A man may hate sin more in others, than in himself. So, the drunkard does this; he hates drunkenness in another, and yet practices it himself! The liar hates falsehood in another, but likes it himself. Now he that hates sin from a principle of grace, hates sin most in himself. He hates sin in others, but he loathes most the sins of his own heart.

3. A man may hate one sin as being contrary to another. There is a great contrariety between sin and sin, between lust and lust; it is the excellency of the life of grace, that it is a uniform life; there is no one grace contrary to another. The graces of God's Spirit are different, but not differing. Faith, and love, and holiness, are all one. They consist together at the same time, in the same subject; no, they cannot be parted. There can be no faith without love, no love without holiness; and so, on the other hand, no holiness without love; no love without faith. So that this makes the life of grace an easy and excellent life. But the life of sin is a distracting contradictious life, in which a man is a servant to contrary lusts. The lust of pride and

prodigality is contrary to the lust of covetousness, *etc.* Now, where one lust gets to be the master-lust of the soul, then that works a hatred of its contrary. Where covetousness gets the heart, there the heart hates pride; and where pride gets uppermost in the heart, there the heart hates covetousness. In this way, a man may hate sin, not from a principle of grace, but from the contrariety of lust. He does not hate any sin, as it is sin; but he hates it, as being contrary to his beloved sin.

Now then, if a man may hate sin for the shame that attends it; if he may hate sin more in others than himself; if he may hate one sin as being contrary to another, then he may hate sin, and yet be but *almost a Christian*.

VI. A man may make great vows and promises; he may have strong purposes and resolutions against sin, and yet be but *almost a Christian*.

Saul did this; he promises and resolves against his sin, "Return, my son David," he says, "for I will no more do thee harm," (1 Sam. 26:21). What promises and resolves did Pharaoh make against that sin of detaining God's people? He says, "I will let the people go, that they may do sacrifice to the Lord," (Exod. 8:28). And again, "I will let ye go, and ye shall stay no longer," (Exod. 9:28). And yet Saul and Pharaoh both perished in their sins. The greatest purposes and promises against sin will not make a man a Christian. *For:*

1. Purposes and promises against sin, never hurt sin. We say, "threatened folks live long;" and truly so do threatened sins. It is not new purposes, but a new nature, that must help us against sin. Purposes may bring to the

birth, but without a new nature, there is no strength to bring forth. The new nature is the best soil for holy purposes to grow in; otherwise, they wither and die, like plants in an improper soil.

2. Troubles and afflictions may provoke us to large purposes and promises against sin for the future. What is more common, than to vow, and not to pay? What is more common to make vows in the day of trouble, which we make no conscience to pay in the day of grace? Many covenant against sin when trouble is on them; and then sin against their covenant, when it is removed from them. It was a brave rule that Pliny, in one of his epistles, gave his friend to live by, "That we should continue to be such when we are well, as we promise to be when we are sick." Many are our sick-bed promises, but we are no sooner well, than we grow sick of our promises.

3. Purposes and resolves against sin for the future, may be only a temptation to put off repentance for the present. Satan may put a man on to good purposes, to keep him from present attempts. He knows whatever we purpose, yet the strength of performance is not in ourselves. He knows, that purposes for the future are a means of putting God off for the present; they are not to be used as a secret way casting off a godly opportunity. That is a notable passage, "Follow me," Christ says, to the two men. Now see what answers they gave to Christ, "Suffer me first to go and bury my father," (Matt. 8:21), says one. This man purposes to follow Christ, only he would stay to bury his father. The other says, "Lord, I will follow thee, but let me first go and bid them farewell which are at my house." I will follow you, but I would only first go and take

my leave of my friends, or set my house in order. And yet we do not find that ever they followed Christ notwithstanding their fair purposes.

4. Nature unsanctified may be so far fashioned on, as to make great promises and purposes against sin.

1st, A natural man may have great convictions of sin, from the workings of an enlightened conscience.

2nd, He may approve of the Law of God.

3rd, He may have a desire to be saved.

Now these three together; the workings of conscience, the sight of the goodness of the Law, a desire to be saved, may bring forth in a man great purposes against sin, and yet he may have no heart to perform his own purposes. This was much like their case when they said to Moses, "Go thou near, and hear all that the Lord our God shall say: and tell thou it to us, and we will hear it, and do it," (Deut. 5:7). This is a fair promise, and so God takes it, "I have heard the words of this people; they have well said all they have spoken." So said, and so done, had been well; but it was better said than done; for though they had a tongue to promise, yet they had no heart to perform it, and God saw this, therefore, he said, "O that there were such an heart in them, that they would fear me, and keep my commandments always, that it might be well with them!" (Deut. 5:29). They promised to fear God, and keep his commandments; but they lacked a new heart to perform what an unsanctified heart had promised. It fairs with men in this case, as it did with that son in the Gospel, that said, he would go into the vineyard, "but went not," (Matt. 21:30).

Now then, if purposes and promises against sin, never hurt sin, if present afflictions may draw out large promises, if they may be the fruit of a temptation, or, if from nature unsanctified surely then a man may promise and purpose much against sin, and yet be but *almost a Christian*.

VII. A man may maintain a strife and combat against sin in himself, and yet be but *almost a Christian*. So Balaam did this when he went to curse the people of God. He had a great strife within himself. "How shall I curse," he says, "whom God has not cursed? or how shall I defy whom the Lord has not defied?" (Num. 23:8). And did not Pilate strive against his sin, when he said to the Jews, "Shall I crucify your king? what evil has he done. I am innocent of the blood of this just man," (Matt. 27:24).

OBJECTION. But you will say, is not this an argument of grace, when there is a striving in the soul against sin? For what should oppose sin in the heart but grace? The apostle makes "the lusting of the flesh against the Spirit, and the Spirit against the flesh," to be an argument of grace in the heart. Now I find this strife in my heart, though the remainders of corruption sometimes break out into actual sins, yet I find a striving in my soul against sin.

Answer. It is true, there is a striving against sin, which is only from grace, and is proper to believers; and there is a striving against sin, which is not from grace, and therefore, may be in them that are not believers. There is a strife against sin in one and the same faculty; the will against the will; the affection against the affection; and this is that which the apostle calls, "the lusting of the flesh against the spirit;" that is, the striving of the unregenerate part against the regenerate; and this is ever in the same faculty, and is proper to believers only (Gal. 5:17).

An unbeliever never finds this strife in himself. This strife cannot be in him; it is impossible, as such; that is, while he is on this side a state of grace. But then there is a striving against sin in diverse faculties; and this is the strife that is in them that are not believers. There, the strife is between the will and the conscience; conscience is enlightened and terrified with the fear of hell and damnation; it is against sin the will and affection, not being renewed, and so, they are given over for sin. And this causes great tugging and combats many times in the sinner's heart. It was in this way with the Scribes and Pharisees. Conscience convinced them of the divinity of Christ, and of the truth of his being the Son of God, and yet a perverse will, and carnal affections, cry out, "Crucify him! Crucify him!" Conscience pleaded for him. He had a witness in their hearts; and yet their wills were bent against him. Therefore, they are said "to have resisted the Spirit," namely, the workings and convictions of the Spirit in their consciences. And this is the case of many sinners. When the will and affections are for sin, and plead for it, conscience is against it, and many times frights the soul from the doing of it. And here men take that which opposes sin in them to be grace, when it is only the work of a natural conscience. They conclude the strife is between grace and sin; it is between the regenerate and unregenerate parts; when, alas! it is no other than the contention of a natural conscience against a corrupt will and affections. And if this is so, then a man may have great strifes and combats against sin in him; and yet be but *almost a Christian*.

5. A man may desire grace, and yet be but *almost a Christian*. So did the five foolish virgins, "Give us of your oil," (Matt. 25:8). What was that but true grace? It was that oil that lighted the wise virgins into the bridegroom's chamber. They do not only desire to enter in, but they desire oil to light them in. Wicked men may desire heaven; desire a Christ to save them; there is none so wicked upon earth, but desire to be happy in heaven. But now here are they that desire grace as well as glory, and yet these are but almost Christians.

OBJECTION. But is it not commonly taught that desires of grace are grace? No, does not our Lord Christ make it so? "Blessed are they that hunger and thirst after righteousness; for they shall be filled," (Matt. 5:6).

Answer. It is true, that there are some desires of grace which are grace, *such as:*

1. When a man desires grace from a right sense of his natural state; when he sees the vileness of sin, and the woeful, defiled, and loathsome condition he is in by reason of sin; and therefore desires the grace of Christ to renew and change him; this is grace. This some make to be the lowest degree of saving faith.

2. When a man joins proportionable endeavors to his desires; he not only wishes for grace, but works for grace; such desires are grace.

3. When a man's desires are constant and incessant, that do not cease but in the attainment of their object; such desires are true grace. They are a part of the

special work of the Spirit. They do really partake of the nature of grace. Now, it is a known maxim, "that which partakes of the nature of the whole, is a part of the whole," the filings of gold are gold. The sea is not more really water, than the least drop; the flame is not more really fire than the least spark.

But though all true desires of grace, are grace yet all desires of grace, are not true. *For:*

1. A man may desire grace, but not for itself, but for something else; not for grace's sake, but for heaven's sake: he does not desire grace, that his nature may be changed, his heart renewed, the image of God stamped upon him, and his lusts subdued in him. These are blessed desires, found only in true believers. The true Christian only can desire grace for grace's sake; but the *almost Christian* may desire grace for heaven's sake.

2. A man may desire grace without proportionable endeavors after grace; many are good at wishing, but bad at working; like the one that lays in the grass on a summer's day, crying out, "O that this were to work?" Solomon says, "The desire of the slothful kills him." How so? "For his hands refuse to labor," he perishes in his desires. The believer joins desires and endeavors together, "One thing have I desired of the Lord, and that will I seek after," (Psalm 27:4).

3. A man's desires of grace may be unseasonable. In this way, the foolish virgins desired oil when it was too late. The believer's desires are seasonable; he desires grace in the season of grace, and seeks in a time when it may be found. "The wise man's heart knows both time and judgment." He knows his season, and has wisdom to

improve it. The silly sinner does all his works out of season and he sends away the seasons of grace, and then desires grace when the season is over. The sinner does everything too late; as Esau desired the blessing when it was too late, and therefore he lost it. Where, if he had come sooner, he would have obtained it. Most men are like Epimetheus, wise too late. They come when the market is done, when the shop is closed, then they have their oil to get. When they lie on their death-beds, then they desire holy hearts.

4. Desires of grace in many are very inconstant and fleeting, like the "morning dew, that quickly passes away," or like Jonah's gourd, that springs up in a night, and withers in a night. They have no root in the heart, and therefore, quickly perish. Now, if a man may desire grace, but not for grace's sake, if his desires may be without endeavors, if a man may desire grace when it is too late, if these desires may be but fleeting and inconstant, then may a man desire grace, and yet be but *almost a Christian*.

5. A man may tremble at the word of God and yet be but *almost a Christian*, as Belshazzar did at the handwriting upon the wall.

OBJECTION. But is not that a note of sincerity and truth of grace, to tremble at the word? Does not God say, "To him will I look that is of a poor and contrite spirit, and trembles at my word?" (Isaiah 66:2).

Answer. There is a two-fold trembling.

1. One is, when the word discovers the guilt of sin, and the wrath of God that belongs to that guilt; this is where conscience is awake, and causes trembling and amazement. So, when Paul preached of righteousness and judgment, it is said *Felix trembled*.

2. There is a trembling which arises from a holy dread and reverence of the majesty of God, speaking in his word; this is only found in true believers, and is that which keeps the soul low in its own eyes. Therefore, make a note how the words run, "To him will I look that is of a poor and contrite spirit, and trembles at my word," (Isa. 66:2). God does not make the promise to him that trembles at the word; for the devils believe and tremble. The word of God can make the proudest, stoutest sinner in the world to shake and tremble, but it is "to the poor and contrite spirit that trembles." Where trembling is the fruit of a spirit broken for sin, and low in its own eyes, there will God look. Now many tremble at the word, but not from poverty of spirit, not from a heart broken for sin, and low in its own eyes; not from a sense of the majesty and holiness of God. And so, notwithstanding they tremble at the word, yet they are but almost Christians.

3. A man may delight in the word and ordinances of God, and yet be but *almost a Christian*. "They take delight in approaching to God." And it is said of that ground, that it "received the word with joy," and yet it was but "stony ground."

OBJECTION. But is it not made a character of a godly man, to delight in the word of God? Does not David say, "He is a blessed man that delights in the Law of the Lord?"

Answer. There is a delighting in the word, which flows from grace, and is a proof of blessedness.

1. He that delights in the word, because of its spirituality, he is a Christian indeed; the more spiritual the

ordinances are, the more does a gracious heart delight in them.

2. When the word comes close to the conscience, rips up the heart, and discovers sin, and yet the soul delights in it notwithstanding; this is a sign of grace.

3. When delight arises from that communion that is to be had with God there, this is from a principle of grace in the soul.

But there may be a delight in the word, where there is no grace.

1. There are many who delight in the word because of the eloquence of the preacher. They do not delight so much in the truth delivered, as in the dress in which they are delivered. In this way, it is said of the prophet Ezekiel, that he was to them "as a very lovely song of one that has a pleasant voice," (Ezek. 33:32).

2. There are very many who delight to hear the word, that yet take no delight to do it. God says of them, "They delight to hear my words, but they do them not," (Ezek. 33:31).

Now then, if a man may delight in the word, more because of the eloquence of the preacher, than because of the spirituality of the matter, if he may delight to hear the word, and yet not delight to do it, then he may delight in the word, and yet be but *almost a Christian*.

VIII. A man may be a member of the church of Christ, he may join himself to the people of God, partake with them in all ordinances, and share of all church privileges, and yet be but *almost a Christian*.

So, the five foolish virgins joined themselves to the wise, and walked together. Many may be members of the church of Christ, and yet not members of Christ, the head of the church. There was a mixed multitude that came up with the church of Israel out of Egypt. They joined themselves to the Israelites, owned their God, left their own country, and yet were in heart Egyptians notwithstanding, "All are not Israel, that are of Israel."

The church in all ages has had unsound members. Cain had communion with Abel; Ishmael dwelt in the same house with Isaac; Judas was in fellowship with the apostles; and so was Demas with the rest of the disciples. There will be some bran in the finest meal. The drag-net of the Gospel catches bad fish as well as good; the tares and the wheat grow together, and it will be so until the harvest.

God has a church where there are no members but such as are true members of Christ, but it is in heaven, it is the "church of the first-born;" there are no hypocrites, nor rotten, unsound professors, none but the "spirits of just men made perfect." All is pure wheat that God lays up in that garner; there the chaff is separated to unquenchable fire.

But in the church on earth the wheat and the chaff lie in the same heap together; the Samaritans will be near of kin to the Jews when they are in prosperity. So, while the church of God flourishes in the world, many will join to it; they will seem like Jews, though they are Samaritans and seem like saints, though yet they are no better than almost Christians.

IX. A man may have great hopes of heaven, great hopes of being saved, and yet be but *almost a Christian*.

Indeed, there is a hope of heaven which is "the anchor of the soul sure and steadfast," it never miscarries, and it is known by four properties.

First, it is a hope that purifies the heart, purges out sin, "He that has this hope, purifies himself even as God is pure," (1 John 3:3). That soul that truly hopes to enjoy God, truly endeavors to be like God.

Secondly, it is a hope which fills the heart with gladness, "We rejoice in hope of the glory of God," (Rom. 5:2).

Thirdly, it is a hope that is founded upon the promise, as there can be no true faith without a promise, so, nor any true hope. Faith applies the promise, and hope expects the fulfilling the promise. Faith relies upon its truth, and hope waits for its good; faith gives interest, hope expects livery and the possession of that heavenly land.

Fourthly, it is a hope that is wrought by God himself in the soul; who is therefore called, "the God of hope," as being the Author as well as the Object of hope. Now, he that has this hope shall never miscarry. This is a right hope; the hope of the true believer, "Christ in you, the hope of glory," (Col. 1:27). But then, as there is a true and sound hope, so there is a false and rotten hope; and this is much more common, as bastard-pearls are more frequently worn than true pearls.

There is nothing more common, than to see men big with groundless hopes of heaven. *As:*

1. A man may have great hope that has no grace; you read of the, "hope of hypocrites," (Job 27:8). The

performance of duties is a proof of their hope; the foolish virgins would never have done what they did, had they thought they should have been shut out after all. Many professors would not be at such pains in duties as they are, if they did not hope for heaven. Hope is the great motive to action. Despair cuts the sinews of all endeavors. That is one reason why the damned in hell cease acting toward an alteration of their state, because despair has taken hold of them. If there were any hope in hell, they would up and be doing there. So that there may be great hope where there is no grace; experience proves this. Formal professors are men of no grace, but yet men of great hopes. Many times you shall find that none fear more about their eternal condition, than they that have most cause of hope, and none hope more than they that have the most cause of fear. As interest in hope may sometimes be without hope, so hope in God may be without interest.

2. A man may hope in the mercy, and goodness, and power of God, without eyeing the promise; and this is the hope of most. God is full of mercy and goodness, and therefore willing to save; and he is infinite in power, and therefore able to save; why, therefore, should I not rest on him?

Now it is presumption, and therefore sin, to hope in the mercy of God, otherwise than by eyeing the promise; for the promise is the channel of mercy through which it is conveyed. All the blessedness the saints enjoy in heaven, is no other than what is the fruit of promise relied on, and hoped for here on earth. A man has no warrant to hope in God, but by virtue of the promise.

3. A man may hope for heaven, and yet not cleanse his heart, nor depart from his secret sins; that hope of salvation that is not accompanied with heart-purification, is a vain hope.

4. A man may hope for heaven, and yet be doing the work of hell; he may hope for salvation, and yet be working out his own damnation, and so perish in his confidences. This is the case of many, like the water-man that looks one way, and rows another; many have their eyes on heaven whose hearts are in the earth. They hope in God, but do not choose him for a portion. They hope in God, but do not love him as the best good, and therefore are likely to have no portion in him, nor good by him. They are likely to perish without him, notwithstanding all their hopes, "What is the hope of the hypocrite, though he has gained, when God takes away his soul?"

Now then, if a man may have great hopes of heaven, that has no grace, if he may hope in mercy, without eyeing the promise, if he may hope without heart-purifying; if he may hope for heaven, and yet do the work of hell, surely then a man may have great hopes of heaven, and yet be but *almost a Christian*.

X. A man may be under great and visible changes, and these fashioned by the ministry of the word, and yet be but *almost a Christian*, as Herod was. It is said, "when he heard John Baptist, he did many things, and heard him gladly," (Mark 6:20). Saul was under a great change when he met the Lord's prophets; he turned into a prophet too. No, it is said, verse 9 of that chapter, that "God gave him another heart," (1 Sam. 10:9). Now, was not this a work of grace? And was not Saul here truly converted? One would think he was; but yet, indeed, he was not. For though it is said, God gave him *another heart*, yet it is not said, that God gave him *a new heart*. There is a great difference between another heart, and a new heart. God gave him another heart to fit him for as a king and ruler, but did not give him a new heart to make him a believer; another heart may make another man, but it is a new heart that makes a new man.

Again, Simon Magus is a great proof of this truth: he was under a great and visible change; of a sorcerer he was turned to be a believer; he left his witchcrafts and sorceries, and embraced the Gospel; was not this a great change? If the drunkard but leaves his drunkenness, the swearer his oaths, the profane person his profaneness, they think this is a gracious change, and their state is now good. Alas! Simon Magus did not only leave his sins, but had a kind of conversion; for, "he believed, and was baptized."

OBJECTION. But is not that man that is changed, a true Christian?

Answer. Not every change makes a man a Christian. Indeed, there is a change, that whoever is under it is a true Christian.

When a man's heart is so changed, as that it is renewed. When old things, "are done away, and all is become new," (2 Cor. 5:17), when the new creature is worked on in the soul, when a man is "turned from darkness to light, from the power of Satan to God," (Acts 26:18), when the mind is enlightened, the will renewed, the affections made heavenly, then a man is a Christian indeed.

But now you must know that every change is not this change. *For:*

1. There is a civil change, a moral change, as well as a spiritual and supernatural change.

Many men are changed in a moral sense, and one may say, they have become new men; but they are in heart and nature still the same men. They are not changed in a spiritual and supernatural sense, and, therefore, it cannot be said of them, they have become new creatures.

Restraining grace may cause a moral change; but it is renewing grace that must cause a saving change. Now, many are under restraining grace, and so changed morally, that are not under the power of saving grace, and so changed savingly.

2. There is an outward change, as well as an inward change. The outward change is often without the inward, though the inward change is never without the outward. A man's heart cannot be sanctified, but it will influence the life; but a man's life may be reformed, and yet never affect or influence the heart.

3. A man may be converted from a course of profaneness, to a form of godliness; from a filthy conversation, to a fair profession; and yet the heart be the same in one and the other. A rotten post may be decorative without, and yet unsound within. It is common to have the "outside of the cup and platter" made clean, and yet the inside foul and filthy.

Now then, if a man may be changed morally, and yet not spiritually, outwardly, and yet not inwardly, from a course of profaneness to a lifeless form of godliness, then

Question 1

a man may be under great and visible changes, and yet be no more than *almost a Christian.*

I do not speak this to discountenance any change, short of that which is spiritual; but to awaken you to seek after that change which is more than moral. It is good to be outwardly renewed, but it is better to be savingly renewed. I know how natural it is for men to take up with anything like a work of conversion, though it is not conversion and resting in that, they eternally perish.

Beloved, let me tell you, there is no change, no conversion, which can stead your souls in the day of judgment, on this side of that saving work, which is worked on the soul by the Spirit of God, renewing you throughout. The sober man, without this change, shall as surely go to hell, as the foolish drunkard. Morality and civility may commend us to men, but not to God. They are of no value in the procurement of an eternal salvation.

A man may go far in an outward change, and yet be not one step nearer heaven, than he that was never under any change; no, he may be, in some sense, further off; as Christ says, the Scribes and Pharisees were further from heaven, with all their show of godliness, than publicans and harlots, in all their sin and uncleanness. Because, resting in a false work, a partial change, we neglect to seek after a true and saving change. There is nothing more common than to mistake our state, and by overweening thoughts, misjudge our condition, and so perish in our own delusions. The world is full of these foolish builders, that lay the foundation of their hopes of eternal salvation on the sand.

Now, my brethren, would you not mistake the way to heaven, and perish in a delusion? Would you not be found fools at last? for none are such fools as the spiritual fool, who is a fool in the great business of salvation. Would you not be fools for your souls, and for eternity? O! then labor after, and pray for, a thorough work of conversion! Beg of God that he would make a saving change in your souls, that ye may be *altogether Christians*! All other changes below this saving change, this heart change, make us but almost Christians.

XI. A man may be very zealous in the matters of religion, and yet be but *almost a Christian*.

Jehu did not only serve God, and do what he commanded him, but was very zealous in his service: "Come with me, and see my zeal for the Lord of hosts!" and yet in all this Jehu was very much a hypocrite. Joash was a great reformer in Jehoiada's time it is said, "He did that which was right in the sight of the Lord, all the days of Jehoiada the priest." But when Jehoiada died, Joash's zeal for God died with him, and he becomes a terrible wretch.

OBJECTION. But the apostle makes zeal to be a note of sound Christianity: "It is good to be zealously affected in good things;" no, it seems to be the non-such qualification for obtaining eternal life; "The kingdom of heaven suffereth violence, and the violent take it by force," (Matt. 11:12).

Answer. It is true, there is a zeal which is good, and which renders the soul highly acceptable to God; a zeal, that never misses of heaven and salvation. Now this is a zeal which is a celestial fire, the true temper and heat of all the affections to God and Christ. It is a zeal wrought and kindled in the soul by the Spirit of God, who first works it, and then sets it on work. It is a zeal that has the word of God for its guide, directing it in working, both in regard of its object and end, manner and measure. It is a zeal that checks sin, and forwards the heavenly life. It is a zeal that makes the glory of God its chief end; which swallows up all by-end, "The zeal of thy house has eaten me up."

But now all zeal is not this kind of zeal. There is a false zeal, as well as a true. Every grace has its counterfeit. As there is fire, which is true heavenly fire, on the altar, so there is strange fire. Nadab and Abihu offered strange fire on God's altar.

There are several kinds of zeal, none of which are true and sound, but false and counterfeit.

I shall give you eight particular instances of this.

First, there is a blind zeal, a zeal without knowledge. "They have a zeal," the apostle says, "but not according to knowledge," (Rom. 10:2). Now as knowledge without zeal is fruitless, so zeal without knowledge is dangerous. It is like wild-fire in the hand of a fool; or, like the devil in the man possessed, that threw him sometimes into the fire, sometimes into the water.

The eye is the light of the body, and the understanding is the light of the soul. Now, as the body, without the light of the eye, cannot go without stumbling; so, the soul, without the light of the mind, cannot act without erring. Zeal without knowledge, is like a delusion in a dark night, that leads a traveler out of his way, into the bogs and mire. This was the zeal of Paul, while he was a Pharisee, "I was zealous towards God, as ye are all this day;

and I persecuted this way unto the death." And again, "I verily thought with myself, I ought to do many things contrary to the name of Jesus of Nazareth." And, "Concerning zeal, persecuting the church." Such a zeal was that in John, "They shall put you out of the synagogue," silence you, you shall not be suffered to preach," yes, the time comes, that whoever kills you, will think that he doth God service," (John 16:2). This is great zeal, but yet it is blind zeal; and that God abhors.

Secondly, there is a partial zeal, in one thing, fire hot, in another thing key-cold; zealous in this thing, and yet careless in another. Many are first-table Christians, zealous in the duties of the first-table, and yet neglect the second. In this way, the Pharisees were zealous in their *Corban*, and yet unnatural to their parents, suffering them to starve and perish. Others are second-table Christians, zealous in the duties of the second-table, but neglect the first; more for righteousness among men, than for holiness towards God. But now he whose religion ends with the first-table, or begins with the second, he is a fool in his profession; for he is but *almost a Christian*.

The woman that was for the dividing the child, was not the true mother; and he that is for dividing the commands, is not a true believer.

Jehu was zealous against Ahab's house, but not so against Jeroboam's calves; many are zealous against sin of opinion, that yet use no zeal against the sins of their conversation.

Now, as we know that the sweat of the whole body is a sign of health, but the sweat of some one part only, shows a distemper, and therefore physicians do reckon such a heat to be symptomatical. So where zeal reaches to every command of God alike, that is a sign of a sound constitution of soul; but where it is partial, where a man is hot in one part, and cold in another, that is symptomatical of some inward spiritual distemper.

Thirdly, there is a misplaced zeal fixed on unsuitable and disproportionable objects. Many are very zealous in trifling things that are not worth it, and trifling in the things that most require it; like the Pharisees that were diligent tithers of mint, anise, and cumin, but neglected the, "weightier matters of the Law; judgment, mercy, and faith," (Matt. 23:23). They had no zeal for these, though very hot for the other; many are more zealous for a ceremony, than for the substance of religion; more zealous for bowing at the name of Jesus, than for conformity to the life of Jesus; more zealous for a holy vestment, than for a holy life; more zealous for the inventions of men, than for the institutions of Christ. This is a superstitious zeal, and usually found in men unconverted, in whom grace never was wrought. Against such men heathens will rise up in judgment. When was it that Paul was so "exceedingly zealous of the traditions of his fathers.," as he says, but only when he was in his wretched and unconverted state? As you may see in the next verses: "But when it pleased God to call me by his grace, then I conferred not with flesh and blood," (Gal. 1:16). Paul had another kind of zeal then, actuated by another kind of principle.

Fourthly, there is a selfish zeal, that has a man's own end for its motive. Jehu was very zealous, but it was not so much for God, as for the kingdom; not so much in obedience to the command, as in design to step into the throne; and therefore, God threatens to punish him for that very thing he commands him to do, "I will avenge the blood of Jezreel upon the house of Jehu," (Hos. 1:4), because he shed that blood, to gratify his lust, not to obey God. So, Simeon and Levi pretend great zeal for circumcision, seem very zealous for the honor of God's ordinances, when in truth their zeal was covetousness, and revenge on the Shechemites.

Fifthly, there is an outside zeal: such was that of the Scribes and Pharisees; they would not eat with unwashed hands, but yet would live in unseen sins; they would wash the cup often, but the heart seldom; paint the outside, but neglect the inside. Jehu was a mighty outside reformer, but he reformed nothing within, for he had a base heart under all. "Jehu took no heed to walk in the Law of the Lord with all his heart," (2 Kings 10:31). Though his fleece was fair, his liver was rotten. Our Lord Christ observes of the Pharisees, "They pray, to be seen of men;" and fast, so "that they may appear to men to fast," (Matt. 23:25).

Sixthly, there is a forensic zeal, that runs out upon others; like the candle in the lantern, that sends all the heat out at the top; or as the lewd woman Solomon mentions, whose "feet abide not in her own house."

Many are hot and high against the sins of others, and yet cannot see the same in themselves; like the Lamiae, that put on their spectacles when they went abroad, but pulled them off within doors.[17]

---

[17] The *Lamiae* was a mythical creature in an old English story that had special enhanced eyes that would be used while it was out in the

Question 1

It is easy to see faults in others, and as hard to see them in ourselves. Jehu was zealous against Baal and his priests, because that was Ahab's sin; but not against the calves of Bethel, because that was his own sin. This zeal is the true character of a hypocrite; his own garden is overrun with weeds, while he is busy in looking over his neighbor's fence.

Seventhly, there is a sinful zeal. All the former may be called sinful from some defect; but this I call sinful in a more special notion, because it is against the life and chief end of religion. It is a zeal, against zeal, that does not fly at profaneness, but at the very power of godliness; not at error, but at truth; and is most hot against the most spiritual and important truths of the times. Where else are the sufferings of men for the truth, but from the spirit of zeal against the truth? This may be called a *devilish zeal*; for as there is the faith of devils, so there is the zeal of devils, "Therefore his rage is great, because he knows his time is short," (Rev. 12:12).

Eighthly, there is a scriptureless zeal, that is not butted and bounded by the word, but by some base and low end. Such was Saul's zeal, when God bids him to destroy Amalek, "and spare neither man nor beast;" when contrary to God's command, he spares the best of the sheep and oxen, under pretense of zeal for God's sacrifice. Another time, when he had no such command, then he killed the Gibeonites "in zeal to the children of Israel and Judah."

---

world, but when it came home, would take the eyes out of her head and hide them in the cupboard, being blind in her own home.

Many a man's zeal is greater then and there, when and where he has the least warrant from God. The true spirit of zeal is bounded by Scripture; for it is for God and the concerns of his glory. God has no glory from that zeal that has no scriptural warrant.

Now then, if the zeal of a man in the things of God may be only a blind zeal, or a partial zeal, or a misplaced zeal, or a selfish zeal, or an outside zeal, or a forensic zeal, or a sinful zeal, or a scriptureless zeal; then it is evident, that a man may be very zealous in the matters of religion, and yet be but *almost a Christian*.

XII. A man may be much in prayer; he may pray often, and pray much; and yet be but *almost a Christian*. So the Pharisees did this, whom yet our Lord Christ rejects as hypocrites.

OBJECTION. But is not a praying-frame an argument of a sincere heart? Are not the saints of God called "the generation of them that seek the face of God?"

Answer. A man is not, therefore, a Christian, because he is much in prayer. I grant that those prayers that are from the workings and sighings of God's Spirit in us; from sincere hearts lifted up to God; from a sense of our own emptiness, and God's infinite fulness; that are suited to God's will, the great rule of prayer; that are for spiritual things, more than temporal; that are accompanied with faith and dependence, such prayers speak that a man is altogether Christian. But now a man may be much in prayer, and yet be a stranger to such prayer; as,

1. Nature may put a man on prayer; for it is a part of natural worship. It may put a child of God on prayer.

Christ, "went and fell on his face, and prayed, saying, O my Father! if it be possible, let this cup pass from me." This was a prayer of Christ which flowed from the sinless strugglings of nature, seeking its own preservation.

2. A man may pray in pretense for a covering to some sin. This the devout Pharisees did, "Woe to you, Scribes and Pharisees, hypocrites! for ye devour widows' houses, and for a pretense make long prayers: therefore ye shall receive the greater damnation," (Mark 12:40). So the Papists seem very devout to pray a rich man's soul out of purgatory; but it is to cheat the heir of much of his estate, under pretense of praying for his father's soul.

3. A man may pray, and yet love sin; as Augustine before conversion prayed against his sin, but was afraid God should hear him, and take him at his word. Now, God does not hear such prayers: "If I regard iniquity in my heart, God will not hear my prayer," (Psa. 66:18).

4. A man may pray much for temporal things, and little for spiritual things; and such are the prayers of most men, crying out most for temporal things. More for, "Who will show us any good?" than for, "Lord, lift upon us the light of thy countenance." David copies out the prayer of such, "That our sons may be as plants, and that our daughters may be as corner-stones, polished after the similitude of a palace: that our garners may be full, *etc.* Happy is the people that is in such a case!" This is the carnal prayer; and this David calls vanity. "They are strange children, whose mouth speaketh vanity," (Psalm 144:11).

5. A man may pray, and yet be far from God in prayer, "This people draw nigh to me with their mouths, and honor me with their lips, but their heart is far from

me," (Mark 7:6). A man may pray, and yet have no heart in prayer; and that God chiefly looks at, "My son, give me thy heart," (Prov. 23:26).

The Jews have this sentence written upon the walls of their synagogues, "Prayer, without the intention of the mind, is but a body without a soul."

It is not enough to be conscionable to use prayer, but we must be conscionable to the use of prayer. Many are so conscientious that they do not dare but pray; and yet so irreligious, that they have no heart in prayer. A common work of God may make a man conscionable to do duties, but nothing less than giving grace in the heart, will make a man conscionable in the doing of them.

6. A man's prayer may be a lie. As a profession without sanctity is a lie to the world, so prayer without sincerity, is a lie to God. It is said of Israel, that they "sought God, and inquired early after him." They were much in prayer, and God calls all but a lie. "Nevertheless, they did flatter him with their mouths, and they lied to him with their tongues, for their heart was not with him," (Psalm 78:37). Psalm 17:1, "Hearken to my prayer, that goeth not out of feigned lips," David says.

7. Affliction and the pressure of outward evils, will make a man pray, and pray much. "When he slew them, then they sought him, and returned, and inquired early after God." The heathen mariners called every man on his God when in a storm. When they fear drowning, then they fall to praying, (Jonah 1:5). Mariners are for the most part not the devoutest, nor addicted very much to prayer. They will swear twice, where they pray once; and yet it is said, "They cry to the Lord in their trouble," and so here you

have a proverb, "He that cannot pray let him go to sea." "They poured out a prayer when thy chastening was upon them."

Now then, if nature may put a man on prayer, if a man may pray in pretense, and design, if a man may pray, and yet love sin, if a man may pray mostly for temporal things, if a man may pray, and yet be far from God in prayer, if prayer may be a lie, or it may be only the cry of the soul under affliction, surely then a man may be much in prayer, and yet be but *almost a Christian*.

OBJECTION. But suppose a man pray, and prevail with God in prayer, surely that is a witness from heaven of a man's sincerity in prayer: now, I pray, and prevail; I ask, and am answered.

Answer. A man may pray, and be answered; for God many times answers prayers in judgment. As God is sometimes silent in mercy, so he speaks in wrath; and as he sometimes denies prayer in mercy, so he sometimes answers in judgment. When men are over-importunate in something their lusts are upon, and will take *no* as a *no*, then God answers in judgment. "He gave them their own desire." They had desired quails, and God sent them. But now mark the judgment, "While the meat was in their mouths, the wrath of God came upon them, and slew them," (Psalm 78:30).

OBJECTION. But suppose a man's affections are stirred much in prayer; how is it then? Is not that a true note of Christianity? Now my affections are much stirred in prayer.

Answer. So was Esau's, when he sought the blessing. "He sought it carefully with tears," (Heb. 12:17).

A man may be affected with his own parts in a duty, while good notions pass through his head, and good words through his lips. Some good motions also may stir in his heart, but they are but sparks which fly out at the tunnel of the chimney, which suddenly vanish; so that it is possible a man may pray, and prevail in prayer; pray, and be affected in prayer; and yet be but *almost a Christian*.

XIII. A man may suffer for Christ in his goods, in his name, in his person; and yet be but *almost a Christian*.

Every man that bears Christ's cross on his shoulders, does not, therefore, bear Christ's image in his soul.

OBJECTION. But does not our Lord Christ make great promises to them that suffer, or lose anything for him? Does he not say, "Every one that has forsaken houses, or brethren, or sisters, or father, or mother, or wife, or children, or lands, for my name's sake, shall receive an hundred fold, and shall inherit everlasting life?" Surely they are true Christians to whom Christ makes this promise!

Answer. There is a suffering for Christ, that is a note of sincerity, and shall have its reward. That is, when a man suffers for a good cause, upon a good call, and with a good conscience, for Christ's sake, and in Christ's strength; when his sufferings are a filling up, "that which is behind of the sufferings of Christ," (Col. 1:24); when a man suffers as a Christian, as the apostle has it, "If a man suffers as a Christian, let him not be ashamed," (1 Peter 4:16), when a man thrusts not himself into sufferings, but stays God's call, such suffering is a proof of integrity.

But now, every suffering for Christ is not suffering as a Christian, *For:*

1. A man may suffer for Christ, for that profession of religion that is upon him; the world hates the show of religion. Times may come, that it may cost a man as dear to wear the livery of Christ, as to wear Christ himself. Alexander had likely to have lost his life for the Gospel's sake, yet he was that Alexander, as is generally judged, that afterwards made shipwreck of faith, and greatly opposed Paul's ministry.

2. A man may suffer for Christ, and yet not have true love to Christ. This is supposed, "Though I give my body to be burned, and have not charity, it profits nothing," (1 Cor. 13:13).

Love to Christ is the only noble ground of suffering; but a man may suffer much on other ends.

1. Out of opinion of meriting by our sufferings, as the Papists; or,

2. Out of vain glory, or for applause among professors. Some have died, that their names might live; or,

3. Out of a Roman resolution, or stoutness of spirit; or,

4. Out of a design of profit, as Judas forsook all for Christ, hoping to mend his market by closing with him; or,

5. Rather to maintain an opinion, than for truth's propagation. Socrates died for maintaining that there was but one God; but whether he died rather for his own opinion, than for God's sake, I think it is no hard matter to determine. In this way, a man may suffer for professing Christ, and yet suffer on wrong principles.

Now then, if a man may suffer for Christ, from the profession that is upon him, or suffer for Christ, and yet not truly love him, then a man may suffer for Christ, and yet be but *almost a Christian*.

XIV. A man may be called of God, and embrace this call, and yet be but *almost a Christian*.

Judas is a famous instance of this truth. He was called by Christ himself, and came at the call of Christ; and yet Judas was but *almost a Christian*.

OBJECTION. But is not the being under the call of God, a proof of our interest in the predestinating love of God? Does not the apostle say, "Whom he predestinated, them he called?" No, does he not say, in the next verse, "Whom he called, them he justified?" No, does God not call all whom he intends to save?

Answer. Though God calls all those that shall be saved, yet all shall not be saved whom God calls. Every man under the Gospel is called of God in one sense or other, but yet every man under the Gospel shall not therefore be saved, "For many are called, but few chosen."

There is a twofold call of God; internal, and external.

1. There is an internal call of God. Now, this call is a special work of the Spirit, by the ministry of the word, by which a man is brought out of a state of nature, into a state of grace, "out of darkness into light, from being vessels of wrath, to be made heirs of life." I grant, that whoever is under this call of God, is called effectually and savingly, to be a Christian indeed. "Every man that has heard and learned of the Father, comes to me," (John 6:45).

2. There is a call of God which a man may have, and yet not be this call. There is an external call of God, which is by the ministry of the word.

Now every man that lives under the preaching of the Gospel, is in this way called. God calls every soul of you to repent, and lay a sure foundation for heaven and salvation, by the word you hear this day.

But now every man that is in this way called, is not therefore a Christian. *For:*

1. Many under the call of God, come to Christ, but are not converted to Christ, have nothing of the grace and life of Christ; such as he, who, when Christ sent out his servants to bid guests to the marriage, came in at the call of Christ, but yet, "had not on the wedding garment," (Matt. 22:11), that is, had none of the grace and righteousness of Jesus Christ.

2. Many that are under the call of the Gospel, come to Christ, and yet afterwards fall away from Christ; as Judas and Demas did. It is said, when Christ preached a doctrine that his disciples did not like, that "from that time many of his disciples went back, and walked no more with him," (John 6:66).

Now then, if many are only under this external call of God; if many that come to Christ are not converted to Christ, but fall away from Christ; then a man may be called of God, and yet be but *almost a Christian.*

XV. A man may have the Spirit of God, and yet be but *almost a Christian.*

Balaam had the Spirit of God given him when he blessed Israel, "Balaam saw Israel abiding in tents, and the

Spirit of the Lord came upon him," (Num. 24:2). Judas had the Spirit, for by the Spirit he cast out devils; he was one of them that came to Christ, and said, "Lord, even the devils are subject to us," (Luke 10:17). Saul had, "Behold, a company of prophets met him; and the Spirit of God came upon him, and he prophesied among them," (1 Sam. 10:10).

OBJECTION. But you will say, "Can a man have the Spirit of God, and yet not be a Christian?" Indeed, the Scripture says, "If any man have not the Spirit of Christ, he is none of his," but surely if any man have the Spirit of Christ, he is his!

Answer. There is a having the Spirit, which is a sure mark of saintship. This is where the Spirit is an effectual prevailing principle of grace and sanctification, renewing and regenerating the heart. It is where the Spirit is a potent worker, "helping the soul's infirmities." Where the Spirit is so as to "abide forever." But now every man that has the Spirit, does not have the Spirit in this manner. *For:*

1. A man may have the Spirit only transiently, not abidingly. The Spirit may be in a man, and yet not dwell in a man. The Spirit is wherever he dwells, but he does not dwell wherever he is; he is in all, but dwells only in the saints. The hypocrite may have the Spirit for a season, but not to abide in him forever.

2. A man may have the Spirit, and yet not be born of the Spirit. Every true Christian is born of the Spirit. A hypocrite may have the gifts of the Spirit, but not the graces. The Spirit may be in him by the way of illumination, but not by way of sanctification; by way of conviction, but not by way of conversion. Though he may have much common grace for the good of others, yet he

may have no special grace for the good of himself; though his profession be spiritual, yet his state and condition may be carnal.

3. A man may have the Spirit only as a Spirit of bondage. In this way, many have the Spirit working only to bondage. "The Spirit of bondage" is an operation of the Holy Ghost by the Law, convincing the conscience of sin, and of the curse of the Law, and working in the soul such an apprehension of the wrath of God, as makes the thoughts of God a terror to him.

This Spirit may be, and often is, without saving grace. This operation of the Spirit was in Cain and Judas. There are none that receive the Spirit of adoption, but they first receive the Spirit of bondage. Yet many receive the Spirit of bondage, that never receive the Spirit of adoption.

4. A man may have the Spirit of God working in him, and yet it may be resisted by him. It is said of the Jews, "They rebelled, and vexed his Holy Spirit," and the same sin is charged upon their children, "Ye stiff-necked, and uncircumcised in heart, ye have always resisted the Holy Ghost; as your fathers did, so do ye," (Acts 7:51). The hypocrite does not retain the Spirit so long as to come up to regeneration and adoption, but quenches his motions, and by this miscarries eternally.

5. A man may have the Spirit, and yet sin that unpardonable sin. He may have the Holy Ghost, and yet sin the sin against the Holy Ghost; no, no man can sin this sin against it, but he that has some degree of it.

The true believer has so much of the Spirit, such a work of it in him, that he cannot sin that sin, "He that is born of God, sins not," (1 John 5:18). In other words, that "sin unto death," for that is what is meant. The carnal professing sinner, he cannot sin that sin, because he is carnal and sensual, not having the Spirit. A man must have some measure of the Spirit that sins this sin. The hypocrite has this. He is said to be "partaker of the Holy Ghost," and he only is capable of sinning the sin against the Holy Ghost.

Now then, if a man may have the Spirit transiently only, not abidingly; if a man may have the Spirit, and yet not be born of the Spirit; if he may have the Spirit only as a Spirit of bondage; if a man may have the Spirit working in him, and yet it may be resisted by him; if a man may have the Spirit and yet sin that unpardonable sin against it; then surely a man may have the Spirit of God, and yet be but *almost a Christian*.

XVI. A man may have faith, and yet be but *almost a Christian*.

The stony ground, that is, those hearers set out by the stony ground, "for a while believed," (Mark 4:16). It is said, that many believed in the name of Christ, yet Christ did not dare "commit himself to them," (John 2:24). Though they trusted in Christ, yet Christ would not trust them; and why? "because he knew all men." He knew they were rotten at the root, notwithstanding their faith. A man may have all faith, to the removing of mountains, and yet be nothing.

OBJECTION. But how can this be, that a man may have faith, and yet be but *almost a Christian*? Does not our Lord Christ promise life eternal and salvation to all that believe? Is not this the Gospel that is to be preached to every creature, "He that believes shall be saved?"

Answer. Though it is true what our Lord Christ says, that "he that believes shall be saved," yet it is as true, that many believe that shall never be saved; for Simon Magus believed; yes, James says, "The devils believe and tremble," (James 2:19). Now, none will say these shall be saved. As it is true, what the apostle says, "All men have not faith," (2 Thess. 3:2), so it is as true, that there are some men that have faith, who are no better for their faith.

You must know, therefore, there is a two-fold *faith:*
1. Special and saving.
2. Common and not saving.

First, 1. There is a saving faith. This is called "faith of the operation of God," (Col. 2:12). It is a work of God's own Spirit in the soul. It is such a faith as rests and casts the soul wholly upon Christ for grace and glory, pardon and peace, sanctification and salvation. It is a united act of the whole soul, understanding, will and affections, all concurring to unite the soul to an all-sufficient Redeemer. It is such a faith as "purifies the heart," and makes it clean; it influences and gives strength and life to all other graces. Now, whoever has this faith, is a Christian indeed; this is the "faith of God's elect." But *then:*

2. There is a common faith, not saving, a fading and temporary faith; there is the faith of Simon Magus, as well as the faith of Simon Peter. Simon Magus believed, and yet he was in the "gall of bitterness, and in the bond of iniquity." Now Simon Magus had more followers than Simon Peter. The faith of most men will at last be found to be no better than the faith of Simon Magus. *For:*

First, the faith of most is but a temporary faith, endures for a while, and then dies and perishes; true and saving faith, such as is the faith of God's elect, cannot die. It may fail in the act, but not in the habit; the sap may not be in the branch, but it is always in the root.

That faith that perishes, that faith a man may have and perish.

Secondly, there is a faith that lies only in generals, not in particulars. There is a general and particular object of faith, so there is a general and particular faith. The general object of faith is the whole Scripture; the particular object of faith is Christ in the promise. Now many have a general faith to believe all the Scripture, and yet have no faith to make particular application of Jesus Christ in the promise. Devils and reprobates may believe the truth of the Scripture, and what is written of the dying and suffering of Christ for sinners; but there are but few that can close up themselves in the wounds of Christ, and by his stripes fetch in healing to their own souls.

Thirdly, there is a faith that is seated in the understanding, but not in the will; this is a very common faith. Many assent to the truth. They believe all the attributes of God, that he is just, holy, wise, faithful, good, merciful, *etc.* But yet they do not rest on him notwithstanding. They believe the commands are true, but yet do not obey them. They believe the promises are true, but yet do not embrace and apply them. They believe the threatenings are true, but yet do not flee from them.

In this way, their faith lies in assent, but not consent; they have faith to confess a judgment, but none to take out execution: by assent they lay a foundation, but never build upon it by application. They believe that Christ died to save them that believe, and yet they do not believe in Christ, that they may be saved.

O! my brethren, it is not a believing head, but a believing heart that makes a Christian; "with the heart man believes to righteousness:" without this our "faith is vain, we are yet in our sins," (1 Cor. 15:17).

Fourthly, there is a faith without experience; many believe the word on hearsay, to be the word of God; but they never felt its power and virtue on their hearts and consciences. Now what good is it to believe the truth of the word, if a man's conscience never felt the power of the word? What is it to believe the truth of the promise, if we never tasted the sweetness of the promise? We are in this case like a man that believes the description others make of strange countries, but never traveled them to know the truth. Or as a patient that believes all the physician says, but yet tries none of his medicines. We believe the word, because we cannot gainsay it; but yet we have no experience of any saving good wrought by the word, and so are but almost Christians.

Fifthly, there is a faith that is without brokenness of heart, that does not avail to melt or soften the heart, and therefore is not true faith; for the least true faith is ever joined with a bending will, and broken heart.

Sixthly, there is a faith that does not transform the heart; faith without fruit, that does not bring forth the new creature in the soul, but leaves it in a state of sin and death. This is a faith that makes a man a sound professor, but not a sound believer; he believes the truth, but not as it is in Jesus; for then it would change and transform him into the likeness of Jesus. He believes that a man must be changed that would be saved, but yet is not savingly changed by believing. In this way, while others believe to salvation, he believes to damnation, for, "his web shall not become a garment; neither shall he cover himself with his work."

Now then, if a man's faith may be but temporary, or may lie only in generals, or may be seated in the understanding only, or may be without experience, or may be without a broken heart, or without a new heart; surely then a man may have faith, he may taste of this "heavenly gift," and yet be but *almost a Christian.*

XVII. A man may go further yet. He may possibly have a love to the people of God, and yet be but *almost a Christian.*

Every kind of love to those who are saints, is not a proof of our saintship. Pharaoh loved Joseph, and advanced him to the second place in the kingdom, and yet Pharaoh was but a wicked man. Ahab loved Jehoshaphat and made a league with him, and married his daughter Athaliah to Jehoram, Jehoshaphat's son, and yet Ahab was a wicked wretch.

But you will say this seems to contradict the testimony of the Scriptures; for that makes love to the saints and people of God, a sure proof of our regeneration, and interest in life eternal, "We know that we have passed from death to life, because we love the brethren," (1 John 3:14). No, the Spirit of God puts this as a characteristic distinction between saints and sinners, "In this the children of God are manifest, and the children of the devil: whosoever doth not righteousness, is not of God, neither he that loveth not his brother," (1 John 4:20). By brethren we do not understand brethren by place, those who are of the same country or nation, such as are called brethren in Rom. 9:3 or Acts 7:23, 25. Nor do we understand brethren by race, those who are descended of the same parents such are called brethren in James 1:2. But by brethren we understand brethren by grace, and supernatural regeneration, such as are the children of God; and these are the brethren whom to love is a sure sign that we are the children of God.

Answer. To this I answer, that there is a love to the children of God, which is a proof of our being the children of God. As for instance, when we love them as such, for that very reason, as being the saints of God, when we love them for the image of God, which appears in them, because of that grace and holiness which shines forth in their conversations; this is truly commendable, to love the godly for godliness sake, the saints for saintship sake, this is a sure testimony of our Christianity. The love of grace in another, is a good proof of the life of grace in ourselves. There can be no better evidence of the Spirit of Christ in us, than to love the image of Christ in others. For this is a certain truth that a sinner cannot love a saint as such; "an Israelite is an abomination to an Egyptian."

There is a contrariety and natural enmity between the two seeds; between the children of the world, and those whom the Father in His eternal love has "chosen out of the world."

It is likeness which is the great ground of love. Now there is the highest dissimilitude and unlikeness between an unregenerate sinner, and a child of God, and therefore a child of God cannot love a sinner as a sinner: "In whose eyes a vile person is condemned." He may love him as a creature; he may love his soul, or he may love him under some relation that he stands toward him. In this way, God loves the damned spirits, as they are his *creatures*, but as fallen angels, he hates them with an infinite hatred. So to love a sinner, as a sinner, this a child of God cannot do; so neither can a sinner love a child of God as a child of God. That he may love a child of God, that I grant, but it is on some other consideration; he may love a person that is holy, not the person for his holiness, but for some other respect. As,

1. A man may love a child of God for his loving, peaceable, courteous deportment to all with whom he converses. Religion beautifies the conversation of a man, and sets him off to the eye of the world. The grace of God is no friend to morose, churlish, unmannerly behavior among men; it promotes an affable demeanor and sweetness to all; and where this is found, it wins respect and love from all.

2. A man may love a saint for his outward greatness and splendor in the world; men are very apt to honor worldly greatness, and therefore the rich saint shall be loved and honored, whilst the poor saint is hated and despised. This is as if a man should value the goodness of his sword by the embroidery of his belt; or his horse for the beauty of his trappings, rather than for his strength and swiftness.

True love to the children of God, reaches to all the children of God, poor as well as rich, bond as well as free, ignoble as well as noble, for the image of Christ is alike, amiable and lovely in all.

3. A man may love a child of God for his fidelity and usefulness in his place: where religion in the power of it taketh hold of a man's heart, it makes him true to all his trusts, diligent in his business, faithful in all his relations; and this obliges respect. A carnal master may prize a godly apprentice or servant that makes conscience of pleasing his master, and is diligent in promoting his interest.

I might instance in many things of the like nature, as charity, beauty, wit, learning, parts, *etc.*, which may procure love to the people of God from the men of the world. But this love is no proof of charity: For,

First, it is but a natural love arising from some carnal respect, or self-ends: that love which is made by the Scripture an evidence of our regeneration, is a spiritual love, the principal loadstone and attraction whereof is grace and holiness; it is a love which embraces a, "righteous man in the name of a righteous man."

2. A carnal man's love to saints, is a limited and bounded love; it is not universal "to the seed." Now as in sin, he that does not make conscience of every sin, makes conscience of no sin as sin; so he who does not love all in whom the image of Christ is found, loves no one for the image of Christ which is found in them.

Now then, if the love we bear to the people of God may possibly arise from natural love only, or from some carnal respect; or if it be a limited love, not extended to all the people of God, then it is possible that a man may love the people of God, and yet be no better than *almost a Christian*.

XVIII. A man may obey the commands of God, yes, many of the commands of God, and yet be but *almost a Christian*.

Balaam seems very conscientious of steering his course by the compass of God's command. When Balak sent to him to come and curse the people of God, Balaam says, "If Balak would give me his house full of silver and gold, I cannot go beyond the word of the Lord my God." and so he says, "The word that God putteth in my mouth, that shall I speak," (Num. 22:38). The young man went far in obedience, "All these have I observed from my youth up," (Mark 10:20), and yet he was but a hypocrite, for he forsook Christ after all.

OBJECTION. But is it not said, "He that has my commandments, and keepeth them, he it is that loveth me; and he that loveth me shall be loved of my Father; and I will love him, and manifest myself unto him?" And does not our Lord Christ tell us expressly, "Ye are my friends, if ye do whatever I command you?" (John 14:21). And can a man be a friend of Christ and be but *almost a Christian*?

I answer, there is an obedience to the commands of Christ, which is a sure proof of our Christianity and friendship to Christ.

This obedience has a threefold property.

It is, 1. Evangelical. 2. Universal. 3. Continual.

First, it is evangelical obedience, and that both in matter and manner, ground and end.

In its matter, and that is what God requires, "Ye are my friends, if ye do whatever I command you," (John 15:14).

Question 1

In its manner, and that is according as God requires, "God is a Spirit, and they that worship him, must worship him in spirit and in truth," (John 4:24).

In its ground, and that is, "a pure heart, a good conscience, and a faith unfeigned," (1 Tim. 1:5).

In its end; and that is, the honor and glory of God: "Whatever ye do, do all to the glory of God," (1 Cor. 10:31).

Secondly, it is a universal obedience, which extends itself to all the commands of God alike. It respects the duties of both tables. Such was the obedience of Caleb, "who followed the Lord fully;" and of David, who had "respect to all his commands."

Thirdly, it is a continual obedience, a putting the hand to God's plough, without looking back: "I have inclined my heart to perform thy statutes always, even to the end," (Psalm 119:112).

He that in this way obeys the command of God, is a Christian indeed; a friend of Christ indeed. But all obedience to the commands of God, is not this obedience. *For:*

1. There is a partial obedience; a piece-meal religion, when a man obeys God in one command, and not in another; owns him in one duty, and not in another; when a man seems to make conscience of the duties of one table, and not of the duties of another. This is the religion of most.

Now this obedience is no obedience; for as he that does not love God above all, does not love God at all; so he that does not obey all the commands universally, cannot be said to obey any command truly. It is said of those in Samaria that they "feared the Lord, and served their own gods after their own manner," (2 Kings 17:33). And yet in the very next verse it is said, "They feared not the Lord;" so that their fear of the Lord was no fear. In like manner, that obedience to God is no obedience, which is but a partial and piecemeal obedience.

2. A man may obey much, and yet be in his old nature; and if so, then all his obedience in that estate is but a painted sin, "He that offereth an oblation, is as if he offered swine's blood; and he that burneth incense, as if he blessed an idol," (Isa. 66:3). The nature must be renewed, before the command can be rightly obeyed; for "a corrupt tree cannot bring forth good fruit," (Matt. 7:18). Whatever a man's performances are, they cannot be called obedience while the heart remains unregenerate, because the principle is false and unsound. Every duty done by a believer, is accepted of God, as part of his obedience to the will of God, though it be done in much weakness; because, though the believer's hand is weak, yet "his heart is right." The hypocrite may have the most active hand, but the believer has the most faithful and sincere heart.

3. A man may obey the Law, and yet have no love to the Lawgiver. A carnal heart may do the command of God, but he cannot love God, and therefore cannot do it aright; for love to God is the foundation and spring of all true obedience. Every command of God is to be done in love: this is the "fulfilling of the Law." The apostle says, "Though I bestow all my goods to feed the poor, and though I give my body to be burned, (these seem to be acts of the highest obedience), yet if I have not love, it profits me nothing," (1 Cor. 13:3).

Question 1

4. I might add, that a man may be much in obedience from sinister and base selfish ends; as the Pharisees prayed much, gave much alms, fasted much but our Lord Christ tells us, that it was "that they might be seen of men, and have glory of men." (Matthew 6:2). Most of the hypocrite's piety empties itself into vain-glory; and therefore, he is but an empty vine in all he does, because "he bringeth forth fruit to himself." It is the end that justifies the action. Indeed, a good end cannot make a bad action good, but yet the lack of a good end makes a good action bad.

Now then, if a man may obey the commands of God partially, and by halves; if he may do it, and yet be in his natural state; if he may obey the commands of God, and yet not love God; if the ends of his obedience may be sinful and unwarrantable, then a man may be much in obeying the commands of God, and yet be but *almost a Christian*.

XIX. A man may be sanctified, and yet be but *almost a Christian*.

Every kind of sanctification does not make a man a new creature; for many are sanctified that are never renewed. You read of them that "count the blood of the covenant, wherewith they were sanctified, an unholy thing," (Heb. 10:29).

OBJECTION. But does not the Scripture tell us, that "both he who sanctifieth, and they who are sanctified; are all one. for which cause, he is not ashamed to call them brethren." And can a man be one with Christ, and yet be but *almost a Christian?*

Answer. To this I answer; You must know there is a twofold work of sanctification spoken of in Scripture.

The one, common and ineffectual.

The other, special and effectual.

That work of sanctification which is true and effectual, is the working of the Spirit of God in the soul, enabling it to the mortifying of all sin, to the obeying of every command, to "walking with God in all well-pleasing." Now, whoever is in this way sanctified, is one with him that sanctifies. Christ will not be ashamed to call such brethren; for they are "flesh of his flesh, and bone of his bone."

But then there is a more common work of sanctification which is ineffectual as to the two great works of dying to sin, and living to God. This kind of sanctification may help to restrain sin, but not to mortify sin; it may lop off the boughs, but it does not lay the axe to the root of the tree; it sweeps and garnishes the room with common virtues, but does not adorn it with saving graces; so that a man is but *almost a Christian*, notwithstanding this sanctification.

Or in this way, there is an inward and outward sanctification.

Inward sanctification is that which deals with the soul and its faculties, understanding, conscience, will, memory, and affections. Outward sanctification is that which deals with the life and conversation. Both these must concur to make a man a Christian indeed. Therefore, the apostle puts them together in his prayer for the Thessalonians, "The God of peace sanctify you wholly; and, I pray God, your whole spirit, and soul, and body, be preserved blameless unto the coming of our Lord Jesus Christ," (1 Thess. 5:23). A man is then sanctified wholly when he is sanctified both inwardly and outwardly; both in heart and affections, and in life and conversation. Outward sanctification is not enough without inward, nor inward without outward. We must have both "clean hands, and a pure heart." The heart must be pure, that we may not incur blame from within; and the hands must be clean, that we may not incur shame from without. We must have hearts "sprinkled from an evil conscience, and bodies washed with pure water," (Heb. 10:22). "We must cleanse ourselves from all filthiness of flesh and spirit," (2 Cor. 7:1). Inward purity is the most excellent, but, without the outward, it is not sufficient; the true Christian is made up of both.

Now many have clean hands, but unclean hearts. They wash the outside of the cup and platter, when all is filthy within. Now, the former without the latter, profits a man no more than it profited Pilate, who condemned Christ, to wash his hands in the presence of the people: he washed his hands of the blood of Christ, and yet had a hand in the death of Christ. The Egyptian temples were beautiful on the outside, but within you shall find nothing but some serpent or crocodile. "He is not a Jew which is one outwardly." Judas was a saint without, but a sinner within; openly a disciple, but secretly, a devil.

Some pretend to inward sanctity without outward. This is the pretense of the open sinner, "Though I sometimes drop an idle, foolish word," he says, "or though I sometimes swear an oath, yet I think no hurt; I thank God my heart is as good as the best!" Such are like the sinner

Moses mentions; that "blessed himself in his heart, saying, I shall have peace, though I walk in the imagination of mine own heart, to add drunkenness to thirst."

Some pretend to outward sanctity without inward. Such are like the Scribes and Pharisees, "who outwardly appear righteous unto men, but within are full of hypocrisy and iniquity," (Matt. 23:28), fair professors, but foul sinners.

Inward sanctity without outward, is impossible; for it will not reform the life. Outward sanctity without inward, is unprofitable; for it will not reform the heart: a man is not a true Christian without both. The body does not make a man without the soul, nor the soul without the body; both are essential to the being of man, so the sanctification of both, are essential to the being of the new man. True sanctification begins at the heart, but works out into the life and conversation; and if so, then man may attain to an outward sanctification, and yet, for lack of an inward, be no better than *almost a Christian*.

And so I shall end this long pursuit of the almost Christian, in his progress heavenward, with this one general *conclusion:*

XX. A man may do all, as to external duties and worship, that a true Christian can; and, when he has done all, be but *almost a Christian*.

You must know, all the commands of God have *an intra* and *an extra*: there is, as I may say, the body and the soul of the command. And accordingly, there is an internal and an external worship of God.

Now the internal acts of worshipping of God are to love God, to fear God, to delight in God, to trust in God, *etc.*

The external acts of worshipping of God, are by praying, teaching, hearing, *etc.*

Now there is a vast difference between these internal and external acts of worship; and such a difference there is, that they distinguish the altogether from the almost Christian; the sincere believer from the unsound professor: and, indeed, in this very thing the main difference between them lies.

1. Internal acts of worship are good *propter fieri*; the goodness adheres intrinsically to the thing done. A man cannot love God, nor fear God, but it will be imputed to him for a gracious act, and a great part of his holiness. But now, external acts of worship are not denominated good, so much from the matter done, *propter fieri*, as from the manner of doing them. A man cannot sin in loving and delighting in God, but he may sin in praying and hearing, *etc.*, for lack of a due manner.

2. Internal acts of worship put a goodness into external. It is our faith, our love, our fear of God, that makes our duties good.

3. They better the heart, and greater the degrees of a man's holiness. External duties do not always do this. A man may pray, and yet his heart never the holier; he may hear the word, and yet his heart never the softer. But now, the more a man fears God, the wiser he is. The more a man loves God, the holier he is. Love is the perfection of holiness. We shall never be perfect in holiness, until we come to be perfect in love.

4. There is such an excellency in this internal worship, that he who mixes it with his external duties, is a true Christian when he does least but without this mixture, he is but *almost a Christian* that does most.

Internal acts of worship, joined with outward, sanctify them, and make them accepted of God, though few external acts of worship, without inward, make them abhorred of God, though they be never so many. So that, although the almost Christian may do all those duties in hypocrisy, which a true Christian does in sincerity; no, though in doing external duties, he may out-do the true Christian, as the comet makes a greater blaze than the true star; if Elijah fast and mourn, Baal's priests will cut their flesh; yet he cannot do those internal duties, that the meanest true Christian can.

The almost Christian can pray, but he cannot love God; he can teach or hear, *etc.*, but he cannot take delight in God. Mark Job's query concerning the hypocrite, "Will he delight himself in the Almighty?" (Job 27:10). He will pray to the Almighty, but will he *delight* himself in the Almighty? Will he take pleasure in God? Ah, no! He will not; he cannot! Delight in God arises from a suitableness between the faculty, and the object; now, there is none more unsuitable than God and a carnal heart. Delight arises from having what we desire, and from enjoying what we have. How then can he delight in God, that neither enjoys, nor has, nor truly desires God? Delight in God is one of the highest exercises of grace, and therefore, how can he delight in God, that has no grace?

Why, then, should any saint of God be discouraged, when he hears how far the almost Christian may go in the way to heaven. Where, he that is the weakest true believer, that has the least true grace, goes farther than he; for he believes in, and loves God.

Should the *almost Christian* do less, as to the matter of external duties, yet, if he had but the least true faith, the least sincerity of love to Christ, he would surely be saved; and should the true Christian do ten times more duties than he does, yet, if he did not have faith in Christ, and love to Christ, he would surely be rejected.

O! therefore, let not any weak believer be discouraged, though hypocrites may out-do them, and go beyond them in duty; for all their duties are done in hypocrisy, but your faith and love to God in duties, is a proof of your sincerity.

I do not speak this to discourage any soul in the doing of duties, or to beat down outward performances, but to rectify the soul in the doing of them. As the apostle says, "Covet earnestly the best gifts: but yet I show you a more excellent way," (1 Cor. 12:31). So I say, covet the best gifts; covet much to be in duties, much in prayer, much in hearing, *etc.* "But I will show you a more excellent way;" and that is, the way of faith and love. Pray much, but then believe much too. Hear much; read much; but then love God much too. Delight in the word and ordinances of God much, but then delight in the God of ordinances more.

And when you are most in duties, as to your use of them, O then be sure to be above duties, as to your resting and dependence upon them. Would you be Christians, indeed, altogether Christians? O then, be much in the use and exercise of ordinances, but be much more in faith and dependence upon Christ and his righteousness. When your obedience is most to the command, then let your faith be most upon the promise. The professor rests in duties, and so is but *almost a Christian* but you must be sure to rest upon the Lord Christ. This is the way to be altogether Christians; for, if you believe, then are ye Abraham's seed, and heirs according to the promise. And in this way I have answered the first query; in other words, how far a man may go in the way to heaven, and yet be but *almost a Christian.*

    1. He may have much knowledge.
    2. He may have great gifts.
    3. He may have a high profession.
    4. He may do much against sin.
    5. He may desire grace.
    6. He may tremble at the word.
    7. He may delight in the word.
    8. He may be a member of the church of Christ.
    9. He may have great hopes of heaven.
    10. He may be under great and visible changes.
    11. He may be very zealous in the matters of religion.
    12. He may be much in prayer.
    13. He may suffer for Christ.
    14. He may be called of God.
    15. He may, in some sense, have the Spirit if God.
    16. He may have some kind of faith.
    17. He may love the people of God.
    18. He may go far in obeying the commands of God.
    19. He may be, in some sense, sanctified.
    20. He may do all, as to external duties, that a true Christian can, and yet be no better than *almost a Christian.*

Question 2

Why, or where is it, that many men go so far, as that they come to be *almost Christians*?

First, it may be to answer the call of conscience. Though few men have grace, yet all men have conscience. Now do but observe, and you shall see how far conscience may go in this work.

1. Conscience demonstrates that it must own a God, and that this God must be worshipped and served by the creature. We have many atheists in practice; such as the apostle speaks of, "They profess to know God, but in works they deny him," (Titus 1:16). But none can be atheists in judgment. Tully, a heathen, could say, "No nation so barbarous," *etc.* Now there being such a light in conscience, as to discover that there is a God, and that he must be worshipped by the help of further light, the light of the word, a man may be enabled to do much in the ways of God, and yet his heart is without a dram of grace.

2. Know this, that natural conscience is capable of great improvements from the means of grace. Sitting under the ordinances may exceedingly heighten the endowments of conscience. It may be much regulated, though it is not at all renewed. It may be enlightened, convinced, and yet never savingly converted and changed. You read in Hebrews 6:4 of some that were "once enlightened, and tasted of the heavenly gift, and were made partakers of the Holy Ghost." What work shall we call this? It could not be a saving work, a true change and conversion of state; for, notwithstanding this enlightening, and tasting, and

partaking, yet they are here said to fall away, verse 6. Had it been a true work of grace, they could never have fallen away from that. A believer may fall, but he cannot fall away; he may fall foully, but he cannot fall finally, for, "underneath are the everlasting arms," (Deut. 33:27). His faith is established in the strength of that prayer of Christ that our faith "fail not." No, he tells us expressly, that it is eternal life which he gives, from which we shall never perish.

This work, then, here spoken of, cannot be any saving work, because it is not an abiding work; for they that are under it, are said to fall away from it. But though it is not a saving grace, yet it is a supernatural work. It is an improvement made by the word on the consciences of men, through the power of the Spirit. Therefore, they are said to "taste the good word of God," and to be made "partakers of the Holy Ghost." They do not have the Spirit abiding in them savingly, but striving with them, and working upon them convincingly, to the awakening and setting conscience on work. And conscience, in this way stirred, may carry a man very far in religion, and in the duties of the Gospel, and yet be but a natural conscience.

A common work of the Spirit, may steady a man very much in the duties of religion, though it must be a special work of the Spirit that steadies a man to salvation. A man may have the assisting presence of the Spirit, enabling him to preach and pray, and yet he may perish for lack of the renewing presence of the Spirit, enabling him to believe. Judas had the former, and yet perished for need of the latter. He had the Spirit assisting him to cast out devils, but he did not have the Spirit renewing him; for he was cast out himself. In this way, a man may have an improved conscience, and yet be a stranger to a renewed conscience; and conscience, in this way improved, may put a man very much on duty. I pray God, none of us mistake a conscience, in this way improved by the word, for a conscience renewed by the Spirit. The mistake is very easy, especially when a life of duties is its fruit.

3. The conscience of a natural man is subject to distress and trouble. Though a natural conscience is not sanctified with grace, yet it is often troubled at sin. Trouble of conscience is not incident to only believers, but sometimes also to unbelievers. A believer's conscience is sometimes troubled when his sin is truly pardoned. A natural man's conscience is troubled for sin though it is never freed from sin. God sometimes sets the word home on the sinner's conscience, and applies the terrors of the Law to it; and this fills the soul with fear and horror of death and hell. Now, in this case, the soul usually betakes itself to a life of duties, merely to fence trouble out of conscience.

When Absalom sets on fire Joab's cornfields, then he runs to him, though he refused before. So, when God lets a spark of hell, as it were, fall upon the sinner's conscience in applying the terrors of the word, this drives the sinner to a life of duties which he never minded before. The ground of many a man's engaging in religion, is the trouble of his conscience; and the end of his continuing in religion, is the quieting of conscience. If conscience would never check him, God should never hear from him.

Natural conscience has a voice, and speaks aloud many times in the sinner's ears, and tells him, *This ought not to be done. God must not be forgotten, the commands of God ought not to be slighted and living in sin will be the ruin of the soul.* And it is here that a natural man runs to duties, and takes up a lifeless and graceless profession, that he may by this, silence conscience. As a man sick in his stomach, whatever sweet morsel he has eaten, he brings up everything. Although it was sweet while he ate it, yet it is bitter in its rising; so it fares with the sinner when he is sermon-sick, or conscience-sick. Though his sin was sweet in its practice, yet the thought of it rises bitterly on the conscience. Then his profession of religion is the pill he rolls about in his mouth, to take away the bitterness of sin's taste.

4. Natural conscience, enlightened by the word, may discover to a man much of the misery of a natural state; though not effectually to bring him out of it; yet so as to make him restless and weary in it. It may show a sinner his nakedness; and on this the soul runs to a life of duties, thinking by it to stand in the misery of his case, and to make a covering for his nakedness. It is said, "that when Adam and Eve saw they were naked, they sewed fig-leaves together, and made themselves a covering." So when once the sinner sees his nakedness and vileness by reason of sin, where he should run to Christ, and close with him, and beg his righteousness for a covering, "that the shame of his nakedness does not appear," he rather runs to a life of duties and performances, and in this way makes himself a covering with the fig-leaves of a profession, without Christ truly embraced, and conscience at all renewed. Natural man would gladly be his own Savior, and supposes a change of state to be a thing within his own power. And

that the true work of grace lies in leaving off the practice of sin, and taking up a life of duties. Therefore, on this principle, many a graceless professor outstrips a sound believer. For, he rests on his own performances, and hopes these will commend him to God.

Question 3

If a natural conscience may go so far, then what difference is there between this natural conscience in hypocrites and sinners, and a renewed conscience in believers? Or, how may I know whether the working of my conscience is the working of only nature, or else of grace fashioned in it?

Answer. I grant that it is difficult to distinguish between the one and the other; and the difficulty has a twofold rise.

1. It arises from that hypocrisy that is in the best saints. The weakest believer is no hypocrite, but yet there is some hypocrisy in the strongest believer. Where there is most grace, there is some sin; and where there is most sincerity, yet there is some hypocrisy.

Now it is very incident to a tender conscience to misgive and mistrust its state, upon the sight of any sin. When he sees hypocrisy break out in any duty or performance, then he complains, "Surely my aims are not sincere! My conscience is not renewed! It is but natural conscience enlightened, not by grace purged and changed."

2. It arises from that resemblance there is between grace and hypocrisy; for hypocrisy is a resemblance of grace without substance; the likeness of grace, without the life of grace. There is no grace but a hypocrite may have something like it; and there is no duty done by a Christian, but a hypocrite may outstrip him in it. Now, when one that does not have true grace shall go further than one that has, this may well make the believer question whether his grace

Question 3

is true or not; or whether the workings of his conscience are not the workings of nature only, rather than of grace fashioned in it.

But to answer the question, you may make a judgment of this in these seven *particulars:*

1. If a natural man's conscience puts him on duty, he usually bounds himself in the work of God. His duties are limited; his obedience is a limited obedience. He does one duty, and neglects another. He picks and chooses among the commands of God; he obeys one, and slights another. So much is enough, what need is there for any more? If I do thus and thus, I shall go to heaven at last. But now, where conscience is renewed by grace, it is otherwise there. Though there may be many weaknesses which accompany its duties, yet that soul never bounds itself in *working* after God. It never loves God so much, but still it would love him more; nor seeks him so much, but still it would seek him more; nor does it serve God so well at any time, but it still makes conscience of serving him better. A renewed conscience is a spring of universal obedience. It sees an infinite excellency, and goodness, and holiness in God; and therefore, would gladly have its service rise up towards some proportionableness to the object. A God of infinite excellency and goodness, should have infinite love, conscience says. A holy God should have service from a holy heart, conscience says.

Now then, if I set bounds to my love to God, or to my service to God, if I limit myself in my obedience to the holy God, love one command, and slight another, obey in one point, and yet lie cross in another, then all I do is but the workings of a natural conscience. But on the other hand, if I love the Lord with my whole heart, and whole soul, and serve him with all my might and strength, if "I esteem all God's precepts concerning all things to be right, and have respect to all his commands," then is my love and service from a renewed conscience.

2. If a natural man's conscience checks or accuses for sin, then he seeks to stop its mouth, but not to satisfy it. Most of the natural man's duties are to still and stifle conscience.

But now, the believer chooses rather to let conscience cry, than to stop its mouth, until he can do it on good terms, and until he can fetch in satisfaction to it from the blood of Jesus Christ, by fresh acts of faith apprehended and applied. The natural man seeks to still the noise of conscience, rather than to remove the guilt. The believer seeks the removal of guilt by the application of Christ's blood; and then conscience is quiet of itself. As a foolish man, having a chip of wood in his eye, and making it water, he wipes away the water, and labors to keep it dry, but never searches his eye to get out the speck; but a wise man does not mind so much the wiping, as the searching of his eye; something has got in, and that causes the watering, and therefore, the cause must be removed. Now then, if when conscience accuses for sin, I take up a life of duties, a form of godliness, to stop the mouth of conscience; and if on this conscience is still and quiet, then is this but a natural conscience. But if, when conscience checks, it will not be satisfied with anything but the blood of Christ, and therefore I use duties to bring me to Christ, and if I beg the sprinkling of his blood upon conscience, and labor not so much to stop the mouth of it, as to remove guilt from it, then is this a renewed conscience.

3. There is no natural man, let him go never so far, let him do never so much in the matters of religion, but still he has his Delilah, his bosom-lust. Judas went far, but he carried his covetousness along with him. Herod went far; he did many things under the force of John's ministry; but yet there was one thing that he lacked – he did not put away his brother's wife; his Herodias still lay in his bosom. No, commonly, all the natural man's duties are to hide some sin; his profession is only made use of for a cover-shame. But now the renewed conscience hates all sin, as David did: "I hate every false way," (Psalm 119:104). He regards no iniquity in his heart. He uses duties, not to cover sin, but to help work down, and work out sin. Now then, if I profess religion; if I make mention of the name of the Lord, and make my "boast of the Law, and yet through breaking the Law dishonor God," if I live in the love of any sin, and make use of my profession to cover it, then am I a hypocrite, and my duties flow but from a natural conscience. But, on the other hand, if I "name the name of the Lord Jesus, and withal depart from iniquity," if I use duties, not to cover, but to discover and mortify sin; then am I upright before God, and my duties flow from a renewed conscience.

4. A natural man prides himself in his duties. If he be much in duty, then he is much lifted up under duty. So did the Pharisee, "God, I thank thee that I am not as other men are," (Luke 18:11), and why? Where lays the difference? Why, "I fast twice in the week. I give tithes of all," *etc.*

But now take a gracious heart, a renewed conscience, and when his duties are at the highest, then is his heart is at the lowest. So it was with the apostle Paul; he was much in service, "in season, and out of season;" preaching up the Lord Jesus with all boldness and earnestness, and yet very humble, in a sense of his own unworthiness, under all, "I am not worthy to be called an apostle. To me, who am less than the least of all saints, is this grace given, that I should preach among the Gentiles the unsearchable riches of Christ," (Eph. 3:8). And again, "Of sinners, I am chief," (1 Tim. 1:15). So a believer, when he is highest in duties, then is he lowest in humility. Duty puffs up the hypocrite, but a believer comes away humbled; and why? Because the hypocrite has had no visions of God. He has seen only his own gifts and parts, and this exalts him. But the believer has seen God, and enjoyed communion with God, and this humbles him. Communion with God, though it is very refreshing, yet it is also very abasing and humbling to the creature. Jerome observes on Zeph. 1:1, where it is said, that "Cushi was the son of Gedaliah, the son of Amariah;" that "Amariah signifies the "Word of the Lord," Gedaliah signifies the "Greatness of the Lord," and Cushi is interpreted "Humility," or, "my Ethiopian." "So that," he says, "from the Word of the Lord cometh a sight of greatness of the Lord; and from a sight of the greatness of the Lord, cometh humility."

Now then, if I pride myself in any duty, and am puffed up under my performances, then have I not seen nor met with God in any duty. But on the other hand, if when my gifts are at the highest, my heart is at the lowest; if

Question 3

when my spirit is most raised, my heart is the most humbled; if, in the midst of all my services, I can maintain a sense of my own unworthiness, if *Cushi* is the son of *Gedaliah*, then have I seen and had communion with God in a duty, and my performances are from a renewed conscience.

5. Look what that is to which the heart secretly renders the glory of a duty, and that is the principle of the duty. In Hab. 1:16, we read of them that sacrifice to their net, and "burn incense to their drag." Where the glory of an action is rendered to a man's self, the principle of that action is *self*. All rivers run into the sea; that is an argument they came from the sea. So, when all a man's duties terminate in *self*, then is *self* the principle of everything. Now all the natural man's duties run into himself. He was never, by a thorough work of grace, truly cast out of himself, and brought to deny himself, and therefore, he can rise no higher than himself in all he does. He was never brought to be poor in spirit, and so to live on another, to be carried out of all duties to Jesus Christ. But the believer gives the glory of all his services to God; whatever strength or life there is in duty, God has all the glory; for he is by grace *outed* of himself, and therefore sees no excellence or worthiness in *self*.

"I labored more abundantly than they all," (1 Cor. 15:10), the apostle says; but to whom does he ascribe the glory of all this? To self? No, "Yet not I," he says, "but the grace of God which was with me." Whenever the grace of Christ is fashioned in the heart as a principle of duty, you shall find the soul when it is most carried out, with a *Yet not I*, in its mouth. "I live, yet not I; I labored more abundantly than all, yet not I." Self is disclaimed, and Christ most advanced, when it is from grace that the heart is quickened. The twenty-four elders cast their crowns at Christ's *feet*.

There are two things that are very hard: one is, to take the shame of our sins to ourselves, the other is to give the glory of our services to Christ. Now then, if I sacrifice to my own net, if I aim at my own credit or profit, and give the glory of all I do to self, then do I "sow to the flesh," and was never yet cast out of self, but act only from a natural conscience. But if I give the glory of all my strength and life in duty only to God, if I magnify grace in all, and can truly say in all I do, *Yet not I,* then am I truly cast out of self, and do what I do with a renewed conscience.

6. Though a natural conscience may put a man much on service, yet it never presses him to the attainment of holiness. So that he carries an unsanctified heart under all. How long was Judas a professor, and yet he did not have one dram of grace. The foolish virgins, you know, "took their lamps, but took no oil in their vessels;" that is, they looked more after a profession, than after a sanctification. But now, when a renewed conscience puts a man on duty, it is succeeded with the growth of holiness. As grace helps doing of duty, so duty helps in growing of grace; a believer is more holy and more heavenly, by his being much in duties.

Now then, if I am much in a life of duties, and yet a stranger to a life of holiness, if I maintain a high profession, and yet have not a true work of sanctification, if, like children in the rickets, I grow big in the head, but weak in the feet, then have I gifts and parts, but no grace; and though I am much in service, yet I have but a natural conscience. But, on the other hand, if the holiness of my conversation carries a proportion to my profession, if I am not "a hearer of the word only, but a doer of it," if grace grows in seasons of duty, then do I act in the things of God from a renewed conscience.

7. And lastly, if a natural conscience is the spring of duty, why then, this spring runs fastest at first, and so abates, and at last dries up. But if a renewed conscience, a sanctified heart, is the spring of duty, then this spring will never dry up. It will run always, from first to last, and run quicker at last than first, "I know thy works, and the last to be more than the first," (Rev. 2:2). "The righteous shall hold on his way; and he that has clean hands shall be stronger and stronger," (Job 17:9).

QUESTION. But you will say, why does that man abate and languish in his duties, that does them from a natural conscience, more than he that does them from a renewed conscience?

Answer. The reason is, because they grow on a fallible root, a decaying root, and that is nature. Nature is a fading root, and so are all its fruits fading; but the duties done by a renewed conscience, are fruits that grow on a lasting root; and that is Christ. "Gifts have their root in nature, but grace has its root in Christ." Therefore, the weakest grace shall outlive the greatest gifts and parts; because there is life in the root of the one, and not in that of the other. Gifts and grace differ like the leather of your shoe, and the skin of your foot. Make a pair of shoes that have the thickest soles, and if you go much in them, the leather wears out, and in a little time a man's foot comes out to the ground; but now a man that goes barefoot all his days, the skin of his feet does not wear out. Why should not the sole of his foot sooner wear out than the sole of his shoe; for the leather is much thicker than the skin? The reason is, because there is life in the one, and not in the other; there is life in the skin of the foot, and therefore that holds out, and grows thicker and thicker, harder and harder. There is no life in the sole of his shoe, and therefore, that wears out, and becomes thinner and thinner. So it is with gifts and grace. Now then, if I decay and abate, and grow weary of a profession, and fall away at last, if I begin in the spirit, and end in the flesh, then all I did was from a natural conscience. But if I grow and hold out, if I persevere to the end, and my "last works are more than my first," then I act from a renewed conscience.

And in this way I have, in seven things, answered that question, namely, if conscience may go so far in putting a man on duties, then what difference is there between this natural conscience in hypocrites and sinners, and renewed conscience in believers?

And that is the first answer to the main query, namely, "Why is it that many men go so far, as that they come to be almost Christians?" It is to answer the call of conscience.

Secondly, it is from the power of the word under which they live. Though the word does not work effectually on all, yet it has a great power on the hearts of sinners to reform them, though not to renew them.

1. It has a discerning, discovering power, "The word of God is quick and powerful, sharper than any two-edged sword, piercing to the dividing asunder of soul and spirit,

and of the joints and marrow; and is a discerner of the thoughts and intents of the heart," (Heb. 4:12). This is the glass in which every one may see what man he is. As the light of the sun discovers the little particles, so the light of the word, shining into conscience, discovers little sins.

2. The word has the power of a Law. It gives Law to the whole soul; it binds conscience. It is, therefore, frequently called *the Law* in Scripture: "Unless thy Law had been my delights," *etc.* "To the Law and to the testimony," (Psalm 119:92; Isa. 8:20). This is spoken of the whole word of God, which is therefore called a Law, because of its binding power on the conscience.

3. It has a judging power. "The word that I have spoken, the same shall judge him at the last day," (John 12:48). The sentence that God will pass upon sinners hereafter, is no other than what the word passes on him here. The judgment of God, is not a day in which God will pass any new sentence; but it is such a day in which God will make a solemn, public ratification of the judgment passed by the ministry of the word on souls here. This I gather clearly from Matthew 18:18, "Whatsoever ye shall bind on earth, shall be bound in heaven; and whatsoever ye shall loose on earth, shall be loosed in heaven." So that, by bringing a man's heart to the word, and trying it by that, he may quickly know what that sentence is that God will pass on his soul in the last day. For, as the judgment of the word is now, such will the judgment of God be concerning him in the last day.

Indeed, there is a twofold power, further than this, in the word. It has a begetting and saving power. But this is put forth only on some. But the other is more extensive, and has a great causality on a profession of goodness, even among them that have no grace.

A man that is under this threefold power of discerning Law and judgment, that has his heart ransacked and discovered, his conscience bound and awed, his state and sinful condition judged and condemned, may take up a resolution of a new life, and convert himself to great profession of religion.

Thirdly, a man may go far in this course of profession from affectation of applause and credit, and to get a name in the world. As it is said of the Pharisees, they "love to pray in the marketplaces, and in the corners of the streets, to be seen of men." Many are of Machiavel's principle, that the appearance of virtue is to be sought, because, though its use is a trouble, yet its credit is a help. Jerome, in his Epistle to Julian, calls such, "the base bond-slaves of common fame." Many a man has that for credit, that he will not do for conscience; and owns religion more for the sake of lust, than for the sake of Christ. In this way making God's stream to turn the devil's mill.

Fourthly, it is from a desire of salvation. There is in all men a desire of salvation. It is natural to every being to love and seek its own preservation. "Who will show us any good?" This is the language of nature, seeking happiness to itself.

Many a man may be carried so far out in the desires of salvation, as to do many things to obtain it. So did the young man, "Good Master, what good things shall I do, that I may inherit eternal life?" (Luke 18:16). He went far, and did much, obeying many commands, and all out of a desire of salvation. So, then, put these together, and there is an answer to that question.

"The call of conscience; the power of the word; the affectation of credit; and the desire of salvation." These may carry a man so far as to be *almost a Christian.*

Question 4

Where do we find that many are but almost Christians when they have gone so far? What is the cause of this?

Answer. I might multiply answers to this question, but I shall instance in two only, which I judge the most material.

First, it is for need of a right and sound conviction. If a man is not thoroughly convinced of sin, and his heart truly broken, whatever his profession of godliness may be, yet he will be sure to miscarry. Every work of conviction is not a thorough work. There are convictions that are not only natural and rational, but not from the powerful work of the Spirit of God.

Rational conviction is "that which proceeds from the working of a natural conscience, charging guilt from the light of nature, by the help of those common principles of reason that are in all men." This is the conviction you read of in Rom. 2:14-15. It is said that the Gentiles who did not have the Law, yet had their consciences bearing witness, and accusing or excusing one another. Though they did not have the light of Scripture, yet they had convictions from the light of nature. Now, by the help of the Gospel light, these convictions may be much improved, and yet the heart not renewed.

But then there is a spiritual conviction and this is that work of the spirit of God upon the sinner's heart by the word, whereby the guilt and filth of sin is fully discovered, and the woe and misery of a natural state

Question 4

distinctly set home on the conscience, to the dread and terror of the sinner while he abides in that state and condition. And this is the conviction that is a sound and thorough work. Many have their convictions, but not this spiritual conviction.

QUERY. Now you will say, "Suppose I am at any time under conviction, how shall I know whether my convictions are only from a natural conscience, or whether they are from the Spirit of God?"

Answer. I would digress too much to draw out the solution of this question to its just length. I shall, therefore, in five things only, lay down the most considerable difference between the one and the other.

1. Natural convictions reach chiefly to open and scandalous sins. These are sins against the light of nature; for natural conviction can reach no further than natural light. But spiritual conviction reaches to secret, inward, and undiscerned sins; such as hypocrisy, formality, lukewarmness, deadness, and hardness of heart, *etc.*

Observe, then, whether your trouble for sin looks inward as well as outward, and reaches not only to open sins, but to secret lusts, to inward and spiritual sins; and if so, this is a sure sign of the work of the Spirit, because the trouble occasioned by these sins, bears a more immediate relation to the holiness of God, who is the one offended by them; they being such as no one else can see or know.

2. Natural convictions deal only with a man's conversation, not with his state and condition. These are with sins actual, not original. But spiritual conviction reaches to all sins; to sins of heart, as well as sins of life; to the sin of our nature, as well as the sins of practice; to the

sin that is born in us, as well as the sin that is done by us. Where the Spirit of the Lord comes to work effectually in any soul, he holds the glass of the Law before the sinner's eyes, and opens his eyes to look into the glass, and to see all that deformity and filthiness that is in his heart and nature.

The apostle Paul said, "I had not known sin but by the Law," (Rom. 7:7). How can this be true, that he had not known sin but by the Law, when the light of nature discovers sin? It is said of the Gentiles, that not having the Law, they had a Law to themselves. This sin, therefore, that the apostle speaks of, is not to be understood of actual sin, but of original sin, "I had not known the pollution of nature, that fountain of sin that is within; this I had not known but by the Law." And, indeed, this is a discovery that natural light cannot make.

It is true, the philosopher could say, "That lust is the first and chief of all sins." But I cannot think he meant it of original sin, but of the inordinacy of appetite and desire, at most; for I find that the wisest of the philosophers understood nothing of original sin. Hear Seneca, "Sin is not born with thee, but brought in since."[18]

Quintilian says, "It is more marvel that any one man sins, than that all men should live honestly; sin is so against the nature of men." How blind were they in this point! And so was Paul, until the Spirit of the Lord showed it to him by the word, and indeed, this is a discovery proper to the Spirit. It is he that makes the sinner see all the deformity and filthiness that is within; it is he that pulls off all the

---

[18] This is *Pelagianism*. – Editor's note.

sinner's rags, and makes him see his naked and wretched condition. It is he that shows us the blindness of the mind, the stubbornness of the will, the disorderedness of the affections, the searedness of the conscience, the plague of our hearts, and the sin of our natures, and in all this the desperateness of our state.

3. Natural convictions carry the soul out to look more on the evil that comes by sin, than on the evil that is in sin. So that the soul under this conviction is more troubled at the dread of hell, and wrath, and damnation, than at the vileness and heinous nature of sin. But now spiritual convictions work the soul into a greater sensibleness of the evil that is in sin, than of the evil that comes by sin. The dishonor done to God by walking contrary to his will; the wounds that are made in the heart of Christ; the grief that the holy Spirit of God is put to, this wounds the soul more than a thousand hells.

4. Natural convictions are not durable, they "are quickly worn out." They are like a slight cut in the skin, that bleeds a little, and is sore for the present, but is soon healed again, and in a few days not so much as a scar to be seen. But spiritual convictions are durable, they cannot be worn out, they abide in the soul until they have reached their end, which is the change of the sinner.

The convictions of the Spirit are like a deep wound in the flesh, that goes to the bone, and seems to endanger the life of the patient, and is not healed but with great skill, and when it is healed leaves a scar behind it, that when the patient is well, yet he can say, "Here is the mark of my wound, which will never wear out." So, a soul that is under spiritual conviction, his wound is deep, and not to be healed, but by the great skill of the heavenly Physician. And when it is healed, there are the tokens of it remaining in the soul, that can never be worn out; so that the soul may say, "Here are the marks and signs of my conviction still in my soul."

5. Natural convictions make the soul shy of God. Guilt works fear, and fear causes estrangedness. So it was with Adam, when he saw his nakedness he ran away and hid himself from God. Now spiritual convictions do not drive the soul from God, but to God. Ephraim's conviction was spiritual, and he runs to God, "Turn thou me, and I shall be turned," (Jeremiah 31:18). So that there is, you see, a great difference between conviction and conversion, between that which is natural and that which is spiritual, that which is common, and that which is saving. Yes, such is the difference, that though a man has never so much of the former, yet if he be without the latter, he is but *almost a Christian*, and therefore, we have great reason to inquire more after this spiritual conviction. *For:*

1. Spiritual conviction is an essential part of sound conversion. Conversion begins here; true conversion begins in convictions, and true convictions end in conversion. Until the sinner is convinced of sin, he can never be converted from sin. Christ's coming was as a Savior to die for sinners; and the Spirit's coming is to convince us as sinners, that we may close with Christ as a Savior. Until sin is thoroughly discovered to us, interest in the blood of Christ cannot rightly be claimed by us; no, so long as sin is unseen, Christ will be unsought. "They that be whole need not the physician, but they that are sick," (Luke 5:31).

2. Slight and common convictions, when they are but skin-deep, are the cause of much hypocrisy. Slight convictions may bring the soul to clasp about Christ, but not to close with Christ; and this is the guise of a hypocrite. I know no other rise and spring of hypocrisy, like this of slight convictions: this has filled the church of Christ with hypocrites. No, it is not only the spring of hypocrisy, but it is also the spring of apostasy. What was the cause that the seed was said to wither away? It was because it had no deepness of earth. Where there is thorough conviction, there is a depth of earth in the heart, and there the seed of the word grows; but where convictions are slight and common, there the seed withers for lack of depth. So that you see clearly, in this one instance, where it is that many are but almost Christians, when they have gone so far in religion, in other words, for need of sound convictions.

Secondly, and this has a near relation to the former, "It is for lack of a thorough work of grace first fashioned in the heart." Where this is not, all a man's following profession comes to nothing; that scholar is never likely to read well, that will need to improve the basics of his grammar before he is out of his primer. That which is not worked well in the loom, will never wear well, nor wear long. It will do little service. A Christian that does not come well off the loom, that does not have a thorough work of grace in his heart, will never wear well; he will shrink when it gets wet, and never do much service for God. It is not the pruning of a bad tree that will make it bring forth good fruit; but the tree must be made good, before the fruit can be good.

He that takes up a profession of religion with an unbroken heart, will never serve Christ in that profession with his whole heart. If there is not a true change in that man's heart, that yet goes far, and does much in the ways of God, to be sure he will either die a hypocrite or an apostate.

Look, as in nature, if a man is not born well, but prove to be crooked or misshapen in the birth, why, he will be crooked as long as he lives; you may bolster or stuff out his clothes to conceal it, but the crookedness, the deformity still remains. You may hide it, but you cannot help it; it may be covered, but it cannot be cured. So it is in this case. If a man comes into a profession of religion, but is not born rightly, if he is not "begotten of God, and born of the Spirit," if there is not a thorough work of grace in his heart, all his profession of religion will never mend him. He may be bolstered out by a life of duties, but he will be but a hypocrite at last, for lack of a thorough work at first; a form of godliness may cover his crookedness, but will never cure it.

A man can never be a true Christian, nor accepted of God, though in the highest profession of religion, without a work of grace in the heart. *For:*

1. There must be an answerableness in the frame of that man's heart that would be accepted of God, to the duties done by him; the spirit and affections within, must carry a proportion to his profession without; prayer without faith, obedience to the Law given, without fear and holy reverence of the Lawgiver, God abhors. Acts of internal worship must answer the duties of external worship. Now where there is no grace fashioned in the

heart, there can never be any proportion or answerableness in the frame of that man's heart, to the duties done by him.

2. Those duties that find acceptance with God, must be done in sincerity. God does not take our duties by tale, nor judge of us according to the frequency of our performances, but according to the sincerity of our hearts in their performance. It is this that commends both the doer and the duty to God; with sincerity, God accepts the least we do. Without sincerity, God rejects the most we do, or can do. This is that temper of spirit which God highly delights in, "They that are of a froward heart are an abomination to the Lord, but such as are upright in the way are his delight," (Prov. 11:20). The apostle gives it a great epithet; he calls it, in 2 Cor. 1:12, *the sincerity of God*; that is, such a sincerity as is his special work on the soul, setting the heart right and upright before him in all his ways. This is the crown of all our graces, and the condemnation of all our duties. Thousands perish, and go to hell in the midst of all their performances and duties, merely for lack of a little sincerity of heart to God.

Now where there is not a change of state, a work of grace in the heart, there can be no sincerity to God-ward; for this is not an herb that grows in nature's garden. "The heart of man is naturally deceitful and desperately wicked," (Jer. 17:9) more opposite to sincerity than to anything; as things corrupted carry a greater dissimilitude to what they were than to anything else which they never were.

"God made man upright." Now man voluntarily losing this, is become more unlike himself than anything below himself. He is more like a lion, a wolf, a bear, a serpent, a toad, than to a man in innocence. So that it is impossible to find sincerity in any soul until there is a work of grace fashioned there by the Spirit of God; and here it is that a man is but *almost a Christian* when he has done all.

Question 5

What is the reason that many go no further in the profession of religion, than to be almost Christians?

REASON 1. It is because they deceive themselves in the truth of their own condition; they mistake their state, and think it good and safe, when it is bad and dangerous. A man may look on himself as a member of Christ, and yet God may look upon him as a vessel of wrath. As a child of God, by looking more on his sins than his graces, more on his failings than his faith, more on indwelling lusts than renewing grace, may think his case very bad when yet it is very good, "I am black," (Song 1:5), the spouse says; "and yet," Christ says, "O thou fairest among women!" (Song 1:8). So the sinner, by looking more on his duties than his sins, may think he sees his name written in the book of life, and yet be in the account of God a very reprobate.

There is nothing more common than for a man to "think himself something when he is nothing;" and so he "deceives himself." Many a man blesses himself in his interest in Christ, when he is indeed a stranger to him. Many a man thinks his sin pardoned, when alas! "he is still in the gall of bitterness, and bond of iniquity." Many a man thinks he has grace, when he has none. Solomon says, "There is that maketh himself rich, yet hath nothing," (Prov. 13:7). This was the very temper of Laodicea, "Thou sayest, I am rich, and increased with goods, and have need of nothing; and knowest not," (I pray that you mind that,) "that you are wretched, and miserable, and poor, and blind, and naked," (Rev. 3:17). You see that as bad as she was, she thought her state was good; as poor as she was in grace, she thought she was rich; "as miserable and naked as she was, yet she thought she had need of nothing."

Now there are several rises or grounds of this mistake. I will name five to you.

First, the desperate deceitfulness of the heart of every natural man. "The heart is deceitful above all things." The Hebrew word is the same with Jacob's name. Now you know he was a supplanter of his brother Esau: "He is rightly called Jacob," he says, "for he has supplanted one these two times." So the word signifies, to be fraudulent, subtle, deceitful, and supplanting. In this way, is the heart of every natural man "deceitful above all things."

You read of the deceitfulness of the tongue.

And of the deceitfulness of riches.

And of the deceitfulness of beauty.

And of the deceitfulness of friends.

But yet the heart is deceitful *above them all*. No, you read of the deceitfulness of Satan, yet truly a man's heart is a greater deceiver than he; for he could never deceive a man, if his own heart did not deceive him. Now it is from here that a man presumes on the goodness of his case, from the desperate treachery of his own heart.

How common is it for men to boast of the goodness of their hearts! "I thank God, though I do not make such a show and pretence as some do, yet I have as good a heart as the best." O do but hear Solomon in this case: "He that trusteth in his own heart is a fool," (Prov. 28:26). Will any wise man, commit his money to the cut-purse? Will he trust a cheat? It is a good rule, *Remember to distrust*, and it was Augustine's prayer, *That man that trusts to his own heart, shall be sure to find himself deceived at last.*

Secondly, this mistake arises from the pride of a man's spirit; there is a proud heart in every natural man. There was much of this pride in Adam's sin, and there is much of it in all Adam's sons. It is a radical sin, and from here arises this overweening opinion of a man's state and condition. Solomon says, "Be not righteous over much," (Eccl. 7:16). Augustine, speaking occasionally of these words, says, it is "not meant of the righteousness of the wise man, but the pride of the presumptuous man." Now in this sense every carnal man is righteous over much; though he has none of that righteousness which commends him to God, in other words, the righteousness of Christ, yet he has too much of that righteousness which commends him to himself, and that is self-righteousness.

A proud man has an eye to see his beauty, but not his deformity; his parts, but not his spots; his seeming righteousness, but not his real wretchedness. "It must be a work of grace that must show a man the need of grace." The haughty eye looks upward, but the humble eye looks downward, and therefore this is the believer's motto, "The least of saints, the greatest of sinners;" but the carnal man's motto is, "I thank God I am not as other men."

Thirdly, many deceive themselves with common grace instead of saving, through that resemblance that is between them. As many take counterfeit money for current coin, so do too many take common grace for true grace. Saul took the devil for Samuel, because he appeared in the mantle of Samuel. So many take common grace for saving grace, because it is *like* saving grace; a man may be under a supernatural work, and yet fall short of a saving work; the first raises nature, the second only renews nature. Though every saving work of the Spirit is supernatural, yet every supernatural work of the Spirit is not saving; and here many deceive their own souls, by taking a supernatural work for a saving work.

Fourthly, many mistake a profession of religion for a work of conversion, and outside reformation for a sure sign of inward regeneration. If the outside of the cup is washed, then they think everything is clean, though it is never so foul within. This is the common rock that so many souls split on, to their eternal hazard, taking up a form of godliness, but denying its power.

Fifthly, lack of a home application of the Law of God to the heart and conscience, to discover to a man the true state and condition he is in. Where this is lacking, a man will sit down short of a true work of grace, and will reckon his case better than it is. That is a notable passage which the apostle hints concerning himself: "I was alive without the Law once; but when the commandment came, sin revived, and I died," (Rom. 7:9). Here you have an account of the different apprehensions Paul had of his condition with and without the word.

1. Here is his apprehension of his condition without the word: "I was alive," he says, "without the Law." Paul had the Law, for He was a Pharisee; and they had the "form of knowledge, and of the truth of the Law." Therefore, when he says he was "without the Law," you must not take him literally, but spiritually. He was without the power and efficacy of it on his heart and conscience, convincing, and awakening, and discovering sin; and so long as this

was the case, he did not doubt of his state. He was confident of the goodness of his condition. This he hinted when he says, "I was alive," but *then:*

2. Here is his apprehension of his condition with the word, and that is quite contrary to what it was before, "when the commandment came," he says, "then sin revived, and I died." When the word of the Lord came with power on his soul, when the Spirit of God set it home effectually on his conscience, that is meant by the coming of the commandment, "then sin revived, and I died;" that is, I saw the desperateness of my case, and the filthiness of all my self-righteousness. Then, my hope ceased, and my confidence failed; and, as before, I thought myself alive, and my sin dead. So, when God had awakened conscience by the word, then I saw my sin alive and powerful, and myself dead and miserable. So that this is the first reason why men go no further in the profession of religion, than to be almost Christians. It is because they mistake their state, and think it is good when it is not. This mistake is fivefold.

1. A deceitful heart.
2. A proud spirit.
3. Taking common grace for saving.
4. Outward reformation, for true regeneration.
5. Lack of application of the Law of God to the heart and conscience.

REASON 2. It is from Satan's cunning, who, if he cannot keep sinners in their open profaneness, then he labors to persuade them to take up with a form of godliness. If he cannot entice them on in their lusts, with a total neglect of heaven, then he entices them into such a profession as is sure to fall short of heaven. He will consent to the leaving some sin, so as we do but keep the rest; and to the doing of some duties, so as we neglect the rest. No, rather than part with his interest in the soul, he will yield far to our profession of religion, and consent to anything but our conversion, and closing with Christ for salvation: he does not care which way we come to hell, so long as he gets us but there at last.

REASON 3. It is from worldly and carnal policy. This is a great hindrance to many. Policy, many times, enters caveats against piety. Jehu will not part with his calves unless he hazard his kingdom. Among many men there would be more zeal and honesty, were there less design and policy. There is an honest policy that helps religion, but carnal policy hinders it.

We are commanded "to be wise as serpents:" now, "the serpent is the subtlest of creatures." But then we must be as "innocent as doves." If piety is without policy, it lacks security; if policy is without piety, it lacks integrity. Piety without policy is too simple to be safe; and policy without piety is too subtle to be good. Let men be as wise, as prudent, as subtle, as watchful as they will, but then let it be in the way of God; let it be joined with holiness and integrity. That is a cursed wisdom that forbids a man to launch any further out in the depths of religion, than he can see the land, unless he be taken in a storm before he can make safe to shore again.

REASON 4. There are some lusts espoused in the heart, that hinder a hearty close with Christ. Though they bid fair yet they come not to God's terms: "The young man would have eternal life;" and he bid fair for it. A willing obedience to every command but one, but only one; and will not God abate him one? Is he so severe? Will he not come down a little in his terms, when man rises so high? Must man yield all? Will God yield nothing? No, my brethren, he that underbids for heaven, shall as surely lose it, as he that will give nothing for it. He that will not give all he has, part with all for that "pearl of price," shall as surely go without it, as he that never once cheapens it. Not coming up to God's terms is the ruin of thousands of souls; no, it is that on which all that perish, do perish. A naked sinner to a naked Christ; a bleeding, broken sinner, to a bleeding, broken Christ; these are God's terms.

Most professors are like iron between two equal loadstones. God draws, and they propend towards God; and the world draws, and they incline to the world. They are between both. They would not leave God for the world, if they might not be engaged to leave the world for God. But if they must part with everything, with every lust, every darling, every beloved sin; why, then, the spirit of Demas possesses them, and God is forsaken by them.

My brethren, this is the great reason why many that are come to be almost Christians go no further. Some one beloved lust or other hinders them, and after a long and high profession, parts them and Christ forever. They did run well, but here it is that they give out, and after all fall short, and perish to eternity.

So, having answered these five questions, *namely:*

1. How far a man may go in the way to heaven, and yet be but *almost a Christian.*

2. Where is it that a man goes so far as to be *almost a Christian.*

3. If a natural conscience may go so far, then what difference is there between this natural conscience in hypocrites and sinners, and a renewed conscience in believers?

4. When it is that a man is but *almost a Christian*, when he has gone so far.

5. What is the reason men go no further in religion, than to be *almost Christians?*

Application

I proceed now to the *Application*.

INFERENCE 1. That salvation is not so easy a thing as it is imagined to be. This is attested by our Lord Jesus Christ himself, "Strait is the gate, and narrow is the way that leadeth to life, and few there be that find it," (Matt. 7:14). The gate of conversion is a very strait gate, and yet every man that would be saved eternally, must enter in at this strait gate; for salvation is impossible without it: "Except a man be born again," born from above, "he cannot see the kingdom of God," (John 3:3, 5).

Not that this gate is strait simply, and in respect of itself. No; for converting grace is free. The gate of mercy stands open all the day long. In the tenders of Gospel grace, none are excluded, unless they exclude themselves. Christ does not say, "If such and such will come to me, I will not cast them out," but, "him that cometh unto me," no matter who he is, if he has a heart to close with me, "I will in no wise cast him out." He does not say, "If this or that man will, here is water of life for him;" but, "If any man will, let him take the water of life freely," (Rev. 22:17). Christ grudges mercy to none. For, though salvation was dearly purchased for us, yet it is freely proffered us.

So that the gate which leads to life is not strait on Christ's part, or in respect of itself, but it is strait in respect of us, because of our lusts and corruptions, which make the entrance difficult. A needle's eye is big enough for a thread to pass through, but it is a strait passage for a cable rope. Either the needle's eye must be enlarged, or the cable rope must be untwisted, or entrance is impossible. It is this way in this case; the gate of conversion is a very strait passage for a carnal, corrupt sinner to go in at. The soul can never pass through with any one lust beloved and espoused; and, therefore, the sinner must be untwisted from every lust. He must lay aside the love of every sin, or he can never enter in at this gate, for it is a strait gate. And when he is in at this strait gate, he meets with a narrow way to walk in. So, our Lord Christ says, "Narrow is the way that leadeth to life," (Matt. 7:14). And what way is this, but the way of sanctification? "For without holiness no man shall ever see the Lord," (Heb. 12:14).

Now this way of sanctification is a very narrow way, for it lies over the neck of every lust, and in the exercise of every grace, subduing the one, and improving the other; dying daily, and yet living daily; dying to sin and living to God: This is the way of sanctification! And O, how few are there that walk in this way! The broad way has many travelers in it, but this narrow way is like the ways of Canaan in the days of Shamgar. It is said, "In the days of Shamgar, the son of Anath, the highways were unoccupied, and the travelers walked through by-ways," (Judges 5:6). In the Hebrew, it is, "through crooked ways:" the way of holiness is by the most an unoccupied way; so the prophet says, "A way shall there be, and it shall be called the way of holiness, the unclean shall not pass over it; no lion shall be there, nor any ravenous beasts shall go up thereon; but the redeemed shall walk there," (Isa. 35:9). The unclean, and the lion, and the ravenous beast, they are in the crooked ways: none but the redeemed of the Lord walk in the way of the Lord.

Application

It is no wonder, then, that our Lord Christ says of life, that "few there be that find it," when the gate is strait, and the way narrow, that leads to it. Many pretend to walk in the narrow way, but they never entered in at the strait gate; and many pretend to have entered in at the strait gate, but they do not walk in the narrow way.

It is a very common thing for a man to perish on a mistake of his way; to go on in those paths that take hold of hell, and yet hope to find heaven at last. Those twenty parts, fore-mentioned, run into destruction, and yet many choose them, and walk in them as the way of salvation. As many profane and open sinners perish by choosing the way of death, so many formal professors perish by mistaking the way of life. This I gather from what our Lord Christ says "Few there be that find it," which clearly implies what in Luke 22:24 expresses plainly, in other words, that many seek it, many seek to enter in, and yet are not able; many run far, and yet do not "so run as to obtain;" many bid fair for the *pearl of price*, and yet go without it. Hell is had with ease, but the "kingdom of heaven suffers violence," (Matthew 11:12).

INFERENCE 2. If many go so far in the way to heaven, and yet miscarry, O then, what shall be the end of them who fall short of these! If he shall perish who is *almost a Christian*, what shall he do who is not at all a Christian! If he that owns Christ, and professes Christ, and leaves many sins for Christ, may be damned notwithstanding; what then shall his doom be that disowns Christ, and refuses to part with one sin, one lust, one oath for Christ; no, that openly blasphemes the precious name of Christ! If he that is outwardly sanctified shall yet be eternally rejected, what will the case be of such as are openly unsanctified, that do not have only the plague of a bad heart within, but also the plague-sore of a profane life without? If the formal professor must be shut out, surely then the filthy adulterer, swinish drunkard, the deep swearer, the profane Sabbath-breaker, the foul-mouthed scoffer, yes, and every carnal sinner much more. If there is a *woe* to him that falls short of heaven, then how sad is the woe to him who falls short of them that fall short of heaven! Ah, that God would make this an awakening word to sinners that are asleep in sin, without the least fear of death, or dread of damnation!

Use of Examination

Are there many in the world that are almost and yet but almost Christians? Why, then, "it is time for us to call our condition into question, and to make a more narrow scrutiny into the truth of our spiritual estate?" We must find out what it is, whether it is right or not; whether we are sound and sincere in our profession of religion, or not. When our Lord Christ told his disciples, "One of you shall betray me," (Mark 14:18), every one began presently to reflect upon himself; "Master, is it I? Master, is it I?" So should we do, when the Lord shows us from his word, how many there are under the profession of religion that are but almost Christians, we should straightway reflect on our hearts, "Lord, is it I? Is my heart unsound. Am I but *almost a Christian*? Am I one of them that shall miscarry at last? Am I a hypocrite under the profession of religion? Have I a form of godliness without the power?"

There are two questions of very great importance, which we should every one of us often put to *ourselves:*

What am I?

Where am I?

1. What am I? Am I a child of God or not? Am I sincere in religion, or am I only a hypocrite under a profession?

2. Where am I? Am I yet in a natural state, or a state of grace? Am I yet in the old root, in old Adam; or am I in the root Christ Jesus? Am I in the covenant of works that ministers only wrath and death? Or am I in the covenant of grace, that ministers life and peace?

Indeed, this is the first thing a man should look at. There must be a change of state, before there can be a change of heart. We must come under a change of covenant, before we can be under a change of condition; for the new heart and the new spirit is promised in the new covenant of grace in Christ. There is nothing of that to be heard of in the covenant of works. Now a man must be under the new covenant, before he can receive the blessing promised in the new covenant; he must be in a new covenant-state, before he can receive a new covenant-heart. No mercy, no pardon, no change, no conversion, no grace dispensed out of covenant; therefore, this should be our great inquiry; for if we do not know where we are, we cannot know what we are; and if we do not know what we are, we cannot be what we should be; namely, *altogether Christians*. Let me then, I beg you, press this duty on you that are professors. Try your own hearts, "examine yourselves whether you are in the faith; prove your own selves," (2 Cor. 13:5). I urge this on most cogent arguments.

1. Because many rest in a notion of godliness and outward shows of religion, and yet remain in their natural condition. Many "are hearers of the word," but "not doers of it," "and so deceive their own souls." Some neither hear nor do; these are profane sinners. Some both hear and do; these are true believers. Some hear, but they do not do; these are hypocritical professors.

He that slights the ordinances cannot be a true Christian; but yet it is possible a man may own them, and profess them, and yet not be a true Christian. Who would trust to a profession, that shall see Judas a disciple, an apostle, a preacher of the Gospel, one that cast out devils, to be cast out himself? "He is not a Jew who is one outwardly, neither is that circumcision which is outward in the flesh: but he is a Jew which is one inwardly: and circumcision is that of the heart, in the spirit, and not in the letter; whose praise is not of men, but of God," (Rom. 2:28).

2. "Because errors in the first foundation are very dangerous." If we are not right in the main, in the fundamental work, if the foundation is not laid in grace in the heart, all our following profession comes to nothing. The house is built on a sandy foundation, and though it may stand for a while, yet "when the floods come, and the winds blow and beat upon it, great will be the fall of it," (Matt. 7:27).

3. "Because many are the deceits that our souls are liable to in this case." There are many things like grace that are not grace. Now it is the likeness and similitude of things that deceives, and makes one thing to be taken for another. Many take gifts for grace, common knowledge for saving knowledge; where a man may have great gifts, and yet no grace; he may have great knowledge, and yet not have Jesus Christ.

Some take common grace for saving; where, a man may believe all the truths of the Gospel, all the promises, all the threatenings, all the articles of the creed, to be true, and yet perish for lack of saving grace.

Some take morality and restraining grace for piety and renewing grace, whereas it is common to have sin much restrained, where the heart is not renewed.

Some are deceived with a half-work, taking conviction for conversion, reformation for regeneration;

we have many mermaid-Christians. Or, like Nebuchadnezzar's image, head of gold, and feet of clay. The devil cheats most men by a *synecdoche*, putting a part for the whole; partial obedience to some commands, for universal obedience to all. Endless are the delusions that Satan fastens upon souls, for lack of this self-search. It is necessary, therefore, that we try our state, unless we take the shadow for the substance, and embrace a cloud instead of Juno.

4. Satan will try us at one time or other. He will winnow us and sift us to the bottom; and if we now rest in a groundless confidence, it will then end in a comfortless despair. No, God himself will search and try us at the day of judgment especially; and who can abide that trial, that never tries his own heart?

5. Whatsoever a man's state is, whether he is altogether a Christian or not, whether his principle is sound or not, yet it is good to examine his own heart. If he find his heart good, his principles right and sound, this will be matter of rejoicing. If he finds his heart rotten, his principles false and unsound, the discovery is in order to a renewing. If a man has a disease on him, and knows it, he may send to the physician in time; but what a sad vexation will it be, not to see a disease until it be past cure? So, for a man to be graceless, and not see it until it is too late, to think himself a Christian when he is not, and that he is in the right way to heaven, when he is in the ready way to hell, and yet does not know it, until a death-bed or a judgment-day confute his confidence; this is the most irrecoverable misery.

These are the grounds on which I press this duty, of examining our state. O that God would help us in the doing this necessary duty!

QUESITON. You say, "But how shall I come to know whether I am *almost* or *altogether* a Christian? If a man may go so far, and yet miscarry, how shall I know when my foundation is right; when I am a Christian indeed?"

Answer 1. The altogether Christian closes with, and receives Christ upon Gospel terms. True union makes a true Christian. Many close with Christ, but it is on their own terms they take him and own him, but not as God offers him. The terms on which God in the Gospel offers Christ, are, that we shall accept of a broken Christ with a broken heart, and yet a whole Christ with the whole heart. A broken Christ with a broken heart, as a witness of our humility; a whole Christ with a whole heart, as a witness of our sincerity. A broken Christ respects his suffering for sin; a broken heart respects our sense of sin; a whole Christ includes all his offices; a whole heart includes all our faculties. Christ is a King, Priest, and Prophet, and all as Mediator. Without any one of these offices, the work of salvation could not have been completed. As a Priest, he redeems us; as a Prophet, he instructs us; as a King, he sanctifies and saves us. Therefore, the apostle says, "He is made to us a God of wisdom, righteousness, sanctification, and redemption," (1 Cor. 1:30). Righteousness and redemption flow from him as a Priest, wisdom, as a Prophet, sanctification, as a King.

Now many embrace Christ as a Priest, but yet they will not own him as a King and Prophet; they like to share in his righteousness, but not to partake of his holiness; they would be redeemed by him, but they would not submit to him; they would be saved by his blood, but not submit to his power. Many love the privileges of the Gospel, but not the duties of the Gospel. Now these are but *almost Christians*, notwithstanding their close relation with Christ; for it is on their own terms, but not on God's. The offices of Christ may be distinguished, but they can never be divided. But the true Christian owns Christ in all his offices. He does not only close with him as Jesus, but as *Lord Jesus*. He says with Thomas, "My Lord, and my God," (John 20:28). He does not only believe in the merit of his death, but also conforms to the manner of his life. As he believes in him, so he lives to him. He takes him for his wisdom, as well as for his righteousness; for his sanctification, as well as his redemption.

2. The altogether Christian has a thorough work of grace and sanctification wrought in the heart, as a spring of duties. Regeneration is a whole change; "all old things are done away, and all things become new." It is a perfect work, as to parts, though not as to degrees. Carnal men do duties, but they are from an unsanctified heart, and that spoils all. A new piece of cloth never does well in an old garment, for the rent is but made worse. When a man's heart is thoroughly renewed by grace, the mind savingly enlightened, the conscience thoroughly convinced, the will truly humbled and subdued, the affections spiritually raised and sanctified; and when mind, and will, and conscience, and affections, all join issue to help on with the performance of the duties commanded; then is a man *altogether a Christian.*

3. He that is altogether a Christian, looks to the manner, as well as to the matter of his duties. Not only that they be done, but how they are done. He knows the Christian's privileges lie in pronouns, but his duty in adverbs. It must not only be *bonum*, good, but it must be *bene*, that good must be *rightly done*.

Here the almost Christian fails, he does the same duties that others do for the matter, but he does not do them in the same manner; while he minds the substance, he does not regard the circumstance. If he prays, he does not regard faith and fervency in prayer. If he hears, he does not mind Christ's rule, "Take heed how you hear," (Luke 8:18). If he obeys, he does not look to the frame of his heart in obeying, and therefore miscarries in all he does. Any of these defects spoil the good of every duty.

4. "The altogether Christian is known by his sincerity in all his performances." Whatever a man does in the duties of the Gospel, he cannot be a Christian without sincerity. Now, the almost Christian fails in this; for though he does much, prays much, hears much, obeys much, yet he is a hypocrite under everything.

5. He that is altogether a Christian, has an "answerableness within to the Law without." There is a con-naturalness between the word of God and the will of the Christian; his heart is, as it were, the transcript of the Law. The same holiness that is commanded in his word, is implanted in the heart; the same conformity to Christ, that is enjoined by the word of God, is fashioned in the soul by the Spirit of God. The same obedience which the word requires of him, the Lord enables him to perform, by his grace bestowed on him. This is that which is promised in

the new covenant "I will put my Law in their inward parts, and write it in their hearts," (Jer. 31:31ff). Now the writing of his Law in us, is nothing else but his working that grace and holiness in us which the Law commands and requires of us.

In the old-covenant administration, God wrote his Laws only on tables of stone, but not on the heart; and therefore, though God wrote them, yet they broke them; but in the new-covenant administration, God provides new tables. Not tables of stone, but "the fleshly tables of the heart," and writes his Laws there, that there might be a Law within, answerable to the Law without. And this every true Christian has. So that he may say in his measure, as our Lord Christ did, "I delight to do thy will, O my God; thy Law is within my heart." Every believer has a light within him, not guiding him to despise and slight, but to prize and walk by the light without him; the word commands him to walk in the light, and the light directs him to walk according to the word. Moreover, from this impression of the Law on the heart, obedience and conformity to God becomes the choice and delight of the soul; for holiness is the very nature of the new creature. So that if there were no scripture, no Bible to guide him, yet he would be holy, for he has received "grace for grace;" there is a grace within to answer to the word of grace without. Now, the almost Christian is a stranger to this Law of God within; he may have some conformity to the word in outward conversation, but he cannot have this answerableness to the word in inward constitution.

6. The altogether Christian is much in duty, and yet much above duty. He is much in duty, in regard of

performances, much above duty, in regard of dependence. He is much in duty by obeying but much above duty by believing. He lives in his obedience, but he does not live on his obedience, but on Christ and his righteousness. The almost Christian fails in this. He is much in duty, but not above it, but rests in it; he works for rest, and he rests in his works. He cannot come to believe and obey too; if he believes, then he thinks there is no need of obedience, and so casts that off. If he is much in obedience, then he casts off believing, and thinks there is no need of that. He cannot say with David, "I have hoped for thy salvation, and done thy commandments." The more a man is in duty, and the more above it; the more in doing, and more in believing, the more a Christian.

7. "He that is altogether a Christian is universal in his obedience." He does not obey one command and neglect another, do one duty and cast off another; but he has respect to all the commands, he endeavors to leave every sin, and love every duty. The almost Christian fails in this, his obedience is partial and piece-meal; if he obeys one command, he breaks another; the duties that least cross his lust, he is much in; but those that do, he lays aside. The Pharisees "fasted, prayed, paid tithes," *etc.*, but they did not lay aside their covetousness, or their oppression; they "devoured widows' houses," they were unnatural to parents.

8. "The altogether Christian makes God's glory the chief end of all his performances." If he prays, or hears, or gives, or fasts, or repents, or obeys, *etc.*, God's glory is the main end of everything. It is true, he may have something else at the latter end of his work, but God is at the further

end. As Moses's rod swallowed up the magicians' rods, so God's glory is the ultimate end that swallows up all his other ends. Now the almost Christian fails in this, his ends are corrupt and selfish; God may possibly be situated at this end of his work, but self is at the other end; for he that was never truly cast out of himself, can have no higher end than himself.

Now then, examine yourself by these characters, put the question to your own soul. Do you close with Christ on Gospel terms? Is grace in the heart the principle of your performances? Do you look to the manner, as well as the matter of your duties? Do you do all in sincerity? Is there an answerableness within to the Law without? Are you much above duty, when much in duty? Is your obedience universal? Lastly, is God's glory the end of everything? If so, then you are not only almost but *altogether a Christian.*

Use of Caution

O! take heed of being almost, and yet but *almost a Christian!* It is a great complaint of God against Ephraim, that "he is a cake not turned," (Hosea 7:8), that is, half baked, neither raw nor roasted, neither cold nor hot, as Laodicea, "Because you are neither hot nor cold, therefore I will spew thee out of my mouth," (Rev. 3:16). This is a condition that of all others is greatly unprofitable, exceedingly uncomfortable, and desperately dangerous.

First, "It is greatly unprofitable to be but *almost a Christian*," for failing in any one point, will ruin us as surely as if we had never made any attempts for heaven. It is no advantage to the soul to be almost converted; for the little that we lack, spoils the good of all our attainments. The saying goes, "as good never a whit as never the near," or, there is no profit in leaving this or that sin, unless we leave *all sin*. Herod heard John gladly, and did many things, but he kept his Herodias, and that ruined him. Judas did many things, prayed much, preached much, professed much, but yet his covetousness spoiled everything; one sin ruined the young man, that had kept all the commands but one. In this way, he "that offends in one point, is guilty of all," (James 2:10). That is, he that lives willfully and allowedly in any one sin, brings the guilt of the violation of the whole Law of God on his soul, and that on a twofold account.

1. Because he manifests the same contempt of the authority of God, in the willful breach of one, as of all.

2. By allowing himself in the breach of any one command, he shows he kept none of the Law in obedience and conscience to God; for he that hates sin as sin, hates *all* sin, and he that obeys the command as the express will of God, obeys *every* command. And for this cause the least sin, willfully, and with allowance lived in, spoils the good of all our obedience and lays the soul under the whole wrath of God. One leak in a ship will sink her, though she is tight every way else. "Gideon had seventy sons," (Judges 8:30), and but one bastard, and yet that one bastard destroyed all his sons; so may one sin spoil all our services; one lust beloved may spoil all our profession, as that one bastard killed all the sons of Gideon.

Secondly, it is exceedingly uncomfortable as appears in three ways.

1. "In that such a one is hated of God and men." The world hates him because of his profession, and God abhors him because of his dissimulation; the world hates him because he seems good, and God hates him because he does but *seem* so. There is no person that God hates more than the almost Christian, "I would that thou wert either cold or hot;" either all a Christian, or not at all a Christian. "Because you are neither cold nor hot, therefore I will spew thee out of my mouth." What a loathsome expression God uses here, to show what an utter abhorrence there is in him against lukewarm Christians! How uncomfortable then must that condition needs be in which a man is abhorred both of God and man?

2. "It is uncomfortable in regard of sufferings." For being *almost a Christian*, will bring us into suffering: but being but *almost a Christian*, will never carry us through

suffering. In Matt. 13:20-21, it is said, "He that receiveth the seed into stony ground, the same is he that hears the word, and with joy receives it; yet has he not root in himself, but dureth for a while; for when tribulation or persecution ariseth because of the word, by-and-by he is offended."

There are four things observable in these words.

1. That the stony ground may receive the word with joy.

2. That it may for some time abide in a profession of it. He endures for a while.

3. That his profession will expose to suffering; for, make note of it, persecution is said to arise because of the word.

4. This suffering will cause an apostatizing from profession; for that which is here called "offence," is in Luke 8:13, called *falling away,* "which for a while believe, and in time of temptation fall away."

I gather from here, a profession may expose a man as much to suffering as the power of godliness. But without the power of godliness there is no holding out in a profession under suffering. The world hates the show of godliness, and therefore persecutes it; the almost Christian lacks the substance, and therefore, cannot hold out in it.

Now this must necessarily be very uncomfortable to say, *if I profess religion, I am likely to suffer; if I do but profess it, I am never likely to endure.*

3. "It is uncomfortable, in regard of that deceit it lays our hopes under." To be deceived of our hopes causes sorrow as well as shame. He that is but *almost a Christian,* hopes for heaven; but unless he is altogether a Christian, he shall never come there. Now to perish with *hopes* of

heaven, to go to hell by the gates of glory, to come to the very door, and then be shut out, as the five virgins were; to die in the wilderness, within the sight of the promised land, at the very brinks of Jordan; this must necessarily be sad. To come within a stride of the goal, and yet miss it; to sink within sight of harbor; O how uncomfortable is this!

4. "As it is greatly unprofitable, and exceedingly uncomfortable, to be but *almost a Christian*, so it is desperately dangerous." *For:*

1. "This hinders the true work:" A man lies in a fairer capacity for conversion, that lies in open enmity and rebellion, than he that softens himself up in the formalities of religion. This I gather from the parable of the two sons, which our Lord Christ urged to the professing Scribes and Pharisees. "There was a man that had two sons; and he came to one, and said, Go work today in my vineyard. He said, I will not; but afterwards repented and went. And he came to the second, and said likewise; and he said, I go, Sir; but went not," (Matthew 21:28ff). The first represents the carnal, open sinner, that is called by the word, but refuses, yet afterwards repents, and believes. The second represents the hypocritical professor, that pretends much, but performs little. Now mark how Christ applies this parable: "Verily I say unto you, that the publicans and harlots go into the kingdom of God before you."

And upon this account it is better not to be at all, than to be *almost a Christian*; for the *almost* hinders the *altogether*. It is better, in this regard, to be a sinner without a profession, than to be a professor without conversion. For the one lies fairer for an inward change, when the other rests in an outward. Our Lord Christ tells the Scribe, "You are not far from the kingdom of God," (Mark 12:34), yet never like to come there. None further from the kingdom of God than such as are not far from the kingdom of God. As for instance, when there lies but one lust, one sin between a soul and Christ, that soul is not far from Christ. But now, when the soul rests in this nearness to Christ, and yet will not part with that one lust for Christ, but thinks his condition secured, though that lust is not subdued; who is further from the kingdom of God than he? So our Lord Christ tells the young man, "One thing thou lackest." Why he was very near heaven, near being a Christian altogether, he was very near being saved; he tells Christ he had kept all the commands. He lacked but one thing; I say, but one thing. But it was a great thing. That one thing he lacked was more than all things he had, for it was the one thing necessary; it was a new heart, a work of grace in his soul, a change of state, a heart weaned from the world. This was the one thing, and he that lacks this one thing, perishes with his *all things else*.

2. "This condition is so like a state of grace, that its mistake for grace is easy and common;" and it is very dangerous to mistake anything for grace that is not grace; for in that a man contents himself, as if it were grace. Formality often dwells next door to sincerity, and one sign serves both; and so the house may be easily mistaken, and by that means a man may take up his lodging there, and never find the way out again.

What one says of wisdom, (many might have been wise, had they not thought themselves so when they were otherwise) the same I may say of grace; many a formal professor might have been a sincere believer, had he not mistook his profession for conversion, his duties for grace, and so rested in that for sincerity that is but hypocrisy.

8. "It is a degree of blasphemy to pretend to grace, and yet have no grace." I gather this from Rev. 2:9, "I know the blasphemy of them which say they are Jews, and are not," (Rev. 2:9). This place undergoes a variety of constructions. Grotius and Paraeus do not make their blasphemy to lie in their saying they are Jews, and are not; but to lie in the reproaches that these Jews fastened on Christ, calling him impostor, deceiver, one that has a devil, *etc.* Brightman goes another way, and says, this was the blasphemy of these Jews. They retained that way of worship that was abrogated, and thrust on God those old rites and ceremonies that Jesus Christ had abolished, and nailed to his cross, by which they overthrew the glory of Christ, and denied his coming. But I conceive the blasphemy of these Jews to lie in this, that they said they were Jews and were not. A Jew here is not to be taken literally and strictly only, for one of the lineage of Abraham, but it is to be taken metonymically for a true believer, one of the spiritual seed of Abraham, "He is a Jew who is one inwardly;" so that for a man to say he is a Jew when he is not, to profess an interest in Christ when he has none, to say he has grace when he has none, this Christ calls blasphemy.

But why should Christ call this blasphemy? This is hypocrisy; but how may it be said to be blasphemy? Why, he blasphemes the great attribute of God's omniscience, he implicitly denies that God sees and knows our hearts and thoughts; for if a man did believe the omniscience of God, that he searches the heart and sees and knows all within, he would not dare to rest in a graceless profession of godliness. This, therefore, is blasphemy in the account of Christ.

4. "It is dangerous to be *almost a Christian*, in that this stills and serves to quiet conscience." Now it is very dangerous to quiet conscience with anything but the blood of Christ: it is bad being at peace until Christ speak peace. Nothing can truly pacify conscience less than that which pacifies God, and that is the blood of the Lord Christ. Now the almost Christian quiets conscience, but not with the blood of Christ. It is not a peace flowing from Christ's propitiation, but a peace rising from a formal profession, not a peace of Christ's giving, but a peace of his own making. He silences and bridles conscience with a form of godliness, and so makes it give way to an undoing, soul-destroying peace; he rocks it asleep in the cradle of duties, and then it is a thousand to one it never awakes more until death or judgment.

Ah, my brethren, it is better to have conscience never quiet, than quieted any way but by "the blood of sprinkling," (Heb. 12:24), a good conscience unquiet, is the greatest affliction to saints; and an evil conscience quiet, is the greatest judgment to sinners.

5. "It is dangerous to be *almost a Christian*, in respect of the unpardonable sin." The sin that the Scripture says, "can never be forgiven, neither in this world nor in the world to come;" I mean the sin against the Holy Ghost (Matt. 12:31). Now such are only capable of sinning that sin as are but almost Christians. A true believer cannot; the work of grace in his heart, that seed of God which abides in him, secures him against it.

The profane, ignorant, open sinner cannot; though he lives daily and hourly in sin, yet he cannot commit this sin, for it must be from an enlightened mind. Every sinner, under the Gospel, especially sins sadly against the Holy Ghost, against the strivings and motions of the Spirit. He "resists the Holy Ghost;" but yet this is not the sin against the Holy Ghost.

There must be three ingredients to make up that sin.

1st, It must be willful. If we sin willfully after we have received the knowledge of the truth, there remains no more sacrifice for sin.

2d. It must be against light and conviction, after we have received the knowledge of the truth.

3d. It must be in resolved malice. Now you shall find all these ingredients in the sin of the Pharisees, Matt. 12:22. Christ heals one that was "possessed of the devil;" a great work, which all the people wondered at, verse 23. But what say the Pharisees? See verse 24. "This fellow casteth out devils by the prince of devils." Now that this was the sin against the Holy Ghost, is clear; for it was both willful and malicious, and against clear convictions. They could not but see that he was the Son of God, and that this work was a peculiar work of the Spirit of God in him and yet they say, he wrought by the devil! whereupon Christ charges them with this "sin against the Holy Ghost," verses 31-33.[19] Now the Pharisees were a sort of great professors; where I gather this conclusion, that it is the professor of religion that is the subject of this sin; not the open carnal

---

[19] Compare this with Mark 3:23-30.

sinner, not the true believer, but the formal professor. Not the sinner, for he has neither light nor grace; not the believer, for he has both light and grace. Therefore, it is the formal professor, for he has light but no grace. Here, then, is the great danger of being *almost a Christian*; he is liable to this dreadful unpardonable sin.

6. "The being but *almost a Christian*, subjects us to apostasy." He that gets no good by walking in the ways of God, will quickly leave them and walk no more in them. This I gather from Hosea 14:9. "Who is wise, and he shall understand these things? prudent, and he shall know them? for the ways of the Lord are right, and the just shall walk in them, but the transgressors shall fall therein."

"The just shall walk in them." He whose heart is renewed and made right with God, he shall keep close to God in his ways.

"But the transgressor shall walk therein." The word in the Hebrew is *peshangim*, from a word that signifies to *evades*. So that we may read the words thus, "The ways of the Lord are right, and the just shall walk in them; but he that evades (that is, a hypocrite,) in the ways of God, he shall fall therein."

An unsound heart will never hold out long in the ways of God, "He was a burning and a shining light, and ye were willing for a season to rejoice in that light," (John 5:35).

"For a season," for an hour, a short space, and then they left him. It is a notable question Job puts concerning the hypocrite, "Will he delight himself in the Almighty? will he always call upon God?" (Job 27:10).

Almost a Christian

He may do much, but these two things he cannot *do:*

1. He cannot make God his delight.

2. He cannot persevere in duties at all times, and in all conditions.

He will be an apostate at last. The scab of hypocrisy usually breaks out in the plague-sore of apostasy. The ground of conversion is ground a person can stand on; it is *terra firma*. But a graceless profession of religion is a slippery ground, and falling ground. Julian the apostate, was first Julian the professor. I know it is possible a believer may fall, but yet, "he rises again, the everlasting arms are underneath." But when the hypocrite falls, who shall help him up? Solomon says, "Woe to him that is alone when he falls!" (Eccl. 4:10), that is without interest in Christ. Why *woe to him*? For he has none to help him up. If Jesus Christ does not recover him, who can? David fell and was restored, for he had one to help him up; but Judas fell and perished, for he was alone.

7. "This being but *almost a Christian*, provokes God to bring dreadful spiritual judgments upon a man."

Barrenness is a spiritual judgment: now this provokes God to give us up to barrenness. When Christ found the fig-tree that had leaves but no fruit, he pronounces the curse of barrenness upon it: "Never fruit grow on thee more," (Matthew 21:19). And so Ezek. 47:11, "The miry places thereof, and the marshy places thereof, shall not be healed; they shall be given to salt."

A spirit of delusion is a sad judgment. Why, this is the almost Christian's judgment, that receives the truth, but not in its love, "Because they received not the love of the truth, that they might be saved; for this cause God shall send them strong delusions," (2 Thess. 2:10).

To lose either light or sight, either ordinances or eyes, is a great spiritual judgment. Why, this is the almost Christian's judgment. He that does not profit under the means of God, provokes God to take away either light or sight; either the ordinances from before his eyes, or else to blind his eyes under the ordinances.

To have a hard heart, is a dreadful judgment, and there is no hypocrite but he that has a hard heart.

My brethren, it is a dreadful thing for God to give a man up to spiritual judgments! Now this being *almost a Christian*, provokes God to give a man up to spiritual judgments: surely, therefore, it is a very dangerous thing to be *almost a Christian*!

8. "Being almost and but almost Christians, will exceedingly aggravate our damnation." The higher a man rises under the means, the lower he falls if he miscarries. He that falls but a little short of heaven, will fall deepest into hell; he that has been nearest to conversion, being not converted, shall have the deepest damnation when he is judged. Capernaum's sentence shall exceed Sodom's for severity because she exceeded Sodom in the enjoyment of mercy; she received more from God, she knew more of God, she professed much for God, and yet was not right with God. Therefore, she shall be punished more by God. The higher the rise, the greater the fall; the higher the profession, the lower the damnation. He miscarries with a light in his hand. He perishes under many convictions; and convictions never end but in a sound conversion, as in all saints; or in a sad damnation, as in all hypocrites. Praying-

ground, hearing-ground, professing-ground, and conviction-ground, is, of all, the worst ground to perish on.

Now, then, to sum up all under this head.

If to be *almost a Christian* hinders the true work of conversion; if it is easily mistaken for conversion; if it is a degree of blasphemy; if this is that which quiets conscience; if this subjects a man to commit the unpardonable sin; if it lays us liable to apostasy; if it provokes God to give us up to spiritual judgments; and if it is that which exceedingly aggravates our damnation; sure then it is a very dangerous thing to be almost and but *almost a Christian!*

O! labor to be *altogether Christians*, to go further than they who have gone farthest, and yet fall short! This is the great counsel of the Holy Ghost, "So run that ye may obtain," (1 Cor. 9:24). "Give diligence to make your calling and election sure," (2 Peter 1:10).

Use of Exhortation

Do you need any motives to quicken you up to this important duty?

CONSIDERATION 1. "This is that which is not only commanded by God, but that whereunto all the commands of God tend." A perfect conformity of heart and life to God, is the sum and substance of all the commands both of the Old and the New Testament. As the harlot was for the dividing of the child, so Satan is for dividing the heart. He would have our love and affections shared between Christ and our lusts; for he knows that Christ reckons we do not love him at all, unless we love him above all. But God will have all or none, "My son, give me thy heart. Thou shalt love the Lord thy God with all thy heart, with all thy soul, and with all thy might," (Matthew 22:37). Look into the Scripture, and see what that is on which you only stand, and you shall find that God has fixed it on those great duties which alone tend to the perfection of your state as Christians. God has fixed you only on believing; only believe. God has fixed you only on obedience, "Thou shalt worship the Lord thy God, and him only shalt thou serve," (Matt. 4:10). "Only let your conversation be such as becometh the Gospel of Christ," (Phil. 1:27). So that you are only fixed on these two great duties of believing and obeying; both which tend to the perfection of your state as Christians and love to God. Now, shall God command, and shall we not obey? Can there be a higher motive to duty than the authority of the great God, whose will is the eternal rule of righteousness? "O let us fear God, and keep his commandments," (Eccl. 12:13), for this is the whole duty of man!

CONSIDERATION 2. "The Lord Christ is a Savior throughout, a perfect and complete Mediator." He does not shed his blood by halves, nor has he satisfied the justice of God, and redeemed sinners by halves. No, but he went through with his undertaking; he bore all our sins, and shed all his blood. He died to the utmost, satisfied the justice of God to the utmost, redeemed sinners to the utmost, and now that he is in heaven he intercedes to the utmost, and is able to save to the utmost.

It is observed, that our Lord Christ, when he was upon the earth, in the days of his flesh, he fashioned no half-cures; but whomsoever they brought to him for healing, he healed them throughout, "They brought unto him all that were diseased, and besought him that they might only touch the hem of his garment, and as many as touched were made perfectly whole," (Mark 1:32).

O! what an excellent physician is here! There is none like him! He cures infallibly, suddenly, and perfectly!

He cures infallibly. None ever came to him for healing that went without it; he never practiced on any that miscarried under his hand.

He cures suddenly. No sooner is his garment touched, but his patient is healed. The leper, Matt. 8:3, is no sooner touched, but immediately cured; the two blind men, Matt. 20:34, are no sooner touched, but their eyes were immediately opened.

He cures perfectly. "As many as were touched, were made perfectly whole."

Now all this was to show what a perfect and complete Savior Jesus Christ would be to all sinners that would come to him. They should find healing in his blood, virtue in his righteousness, and pardon for all their sins, whatever they were. Look! as Christ healed all the diseases of all that came to him, when he was on earth, so he, pardons all the sins, and heals all the wounds of all those souls that come to him, now he is in heaven. He is a Savior throughout; and shall not we be saints throughout? Shall he be altogether a Redeemer; and shall not we be altogether believers? O, what a shame is this!

CONSIDERATION 3. "There is enough in religion to engage us to be altogether Christians;" and that whether we respect profit or comfort, for grace brings both.

First, "Religion is a gainful thing;" and this is a compelling motive that becomes effectual on all. *Gain* is the god whom the world worships. What will men not do, what will they not suffer for gain? What journeys do men take by land, what voyages by sea, through hot and cold, through fair and foul, through storm and shine, through day and night, and all for gain! Now there is no calling so gainful as this of religion; it is the most profitable employment we can take up. "Godliness is profitable unto all things," (1 Tim. 4:8). It is a great revenue. If it is closely followed, it brings in the greatest income. Indeed, some men are religious for the world's sake; such shall be sure not to gain. But they who are religious for religion's sake, shall be sure not to lose, if heaven and earth can recompense them. For godliness has the promise both of the life that now is, and of that which is to come.

Ah, who would not be a Christian, when the gain of godliness is so great! Many gain much in their worldly calling, but the profit which the true believer has from one hour's communion with God in Christ, weighs down all the gain of the world. "Cursed be that man who counts all the gain of the world worth one hour's communion with Jesus Christ," that noble Marquis, Galeacius Caracciola, says. It is nowhere said in Scripture, "Happy is the man that findeth silver, and the man that getteth fine gold." These are of no weight in the balance of the sanctuary; but it is said, "Happy is the man that findeth wisdom, and the man that getteth understanding; for the merchandise of it is better than the merchandise of silver, and the gain thereof than fine gold," (Prov. 3:13). By wisdom and understanding here, we are to understand the grace of Christ, and so the spirit of God interprets it. "Behold the fear of the Lord, that is wisdom; and to depart from evil is understanding," (Job 28:28). Now of all merchants, he that trades in this wisdom and understanding will prove the richest man. One grain of godliness outweighs all the gold of Ophir. There is no riches like being rich in grace. *For:*

1. This is the most necessary riches; other things are not so. Silver and gold are not so. We may be happy without them. There is but one thing necessary, and that is the grace of Jesus Christ in the heart. Have this, and have all; lack this, and lack all.

2. It is the most substantial gain. The things of this world are more shadow than substance. Pleasure, honor, and profit comprehend all things in this world, and therefore are the carnal man's trinity. The apostle John calls them "the lust of the flesh, the lust of the eyes, and the

pride of life," (1 John 2:16), this, (he says,) is all that is in the world. And truly, if this is all, *all is nothing*, for what is pleasure but a dream and conceit? What is honor, but fancy and opinion? What is profit, but a thing of nothing? "Why wilt thou set thy eyes upon that which is not?"[20] The things of the world have in them no sound substance, though foolish, carnal men call them substance. But now grace is a substantial good; so our Lord Christ calls it, "That I may cause those that love me to inherit substance," (Prov. 8:21), to inherit that which is grace is a reality, but other things are show and fancy.

3. Godliness is the safest gain. The gain of worldly things is always with difficulty, but seldom with safety. The soul is often hazarded in the over-eager pursuit of worldly things; no, thousands do pawn, and lose, and damn their precious souls eternally, for a little silver and gold, which are but the guts and garbage of the earth: "and what is a man profited, to gain the whole world, if he lose his own soul?" (Mark 8:36). But the gain of godliness is ever with safety to the soul; no, the soul is lost and undone without it, and not saved but by the attainment of it. A soul without grace is in a lost and perishing condition. The hazard of eternity is never over with us until the grace of Christ Jesus be sought by us, and fashioned in us.

4. "Godliness is the surest profit:" as it is safe, so it is sure. Men make great ventures for the world, but all runs upon uncertainty. Many venture much, and wait long, and yet find no return but disappointment. They sow much, and yet reap nothing. But the gain of godliness is sure, "to

---

[20] See Isaiah 55:1ff.

him that soweth righteousness shall be a sure reward," (Proverbs 11:18).

And as the things of this world are uncertain in the getting, so they are uncertain in the keeping. If men do not undo us, moths may; if robbery does not, rust may; if rust does not, fire may; to which all earthly treasures are incident, as our Lord Christ teaches us in Matt. 6:19. Solomon draws the world with wings, "Riches make themselves wings, and fly as an eagle towards heaven," (Proverbs 23:5). A man may be rich as Dives[21] today, and yet poor as Lazarus tomorrow. O how uncertain are all worldly things! But now the true treasure of grace is in the heart, that can never be lost. It is out of the reach both of rut and robber. "He that gets the world, gets a good he can never keep; but he that gets grace, gets a good he shall never lose."

5. "The profit of godliness does not lie only in this world, but in the world to come." All other profit lies only in this world. Riches and honor, *etc.*, are called this world's goods, but the riches of godliness is chiefly in the other world's goods. These are all found in the enjoyment of God, and Jesus Christ, and the Holy Spirit, among saints and angels in glory. Lo, this is the gain of godliness; "such honor have all his saints."

6. "The gain of godliness is a durable and eternal gain." All this world's goods are perishing; perishing pleasures, perishing honors, perishing profits, and perishing comforts. "Riches are not forever," Job says,

---

[21] In the parable of the Rich man and Lazarus, the old writers referred to the Rich man as Dives, a Latin designation for *rich*.

"Hast thou entered into the treasures of the snow?" (Job 38:22). On these words Gregory observes that earthly treasures are treasures of snow. What pains do children take to scrape and roll the snow together to make a snowball, which is no sooner done but the heat of the sun dissolves it, and it comes to nothing? Why, the treasures of worldly men are but treasures of snow. When death and judgment come, they melt away, and come to nothing. "Riches profit not in the day of wrath, but righteousness delivers from death," (Prov. 11:4).

You see here the great advantage of godliness; so that if we look at profit, we shall find enough in religion to engage us to be altogether Christians. *Or,*

2. "If we look at comfort," religion is the most comfortable profession. There are no comforts to be compared to the comforts of grace and godliness.

1. "Worldly comfort is only outward;" it is but skin-deep. "In the midst of laughter the heart is sorrowful," (Prov. 14:13). But now the comfort that flows from godliness is an inward comfort, a spiritual joy; therefore, it is called gladness of heart. "Thou hast put gladness in my heart," (Psalm 4:7). Other joy smooths the brow, but this fills the breast.

2. "Worldly comfort has a nether spring." The spring of worldly comfort is in the creature, in some earthly enjoyment; and, therefore, the comfort of worldly men must needs be mixed and muddy. "An unclean fountain cannot send forth pure water." But spiritual comfort has an upper spring. The comfort that accompanies godliness, flows from the manifestations of the love of God in Christ, from the workings of the blessed

Spirit in the heart, which is first a counselor, and then a comforter. And therefore, the comforts of the saints must needs be pure and unmixed comforts; for they flow from a pure spring.

3. "Worldly comfort is very fading and transitory." "The triumphing of the wicked is but short, and the joy of the hypocrite is but for a moment." Solomon compares it to the "crackling of thorns under a pot," (Eccl. 7:6), which is but a blaze, and soon out. So is the comfort of carnal hearts. But, now the comfort of godliness is a durable and abiding comfort; "your heart shall rejoice, and your joy no man shall take from you." The comfort of godliness is lasting, and everlasting it abides by us in life, in death, and after death.

First, "It abides by us in life." Grace and peace go together. Godliness naturally brings forth comfort and peace. "The effect of righteousness shall be peace," (Isa. 32:17). It is said of the primitive Christians, "They walked in the fear of the Lord, and in the comfort of the Holy Ghost," (Acts 9:31). Every duty done in uprightness and sincerity, reflects some comfort upon the soul. "In keeping the commands, there is great reward," (Psa. 19:11), not only for keeping of them, but in keeping of them. As every flower, so every duty carries sweetness and refreshing with it.

OBJECTION. "But who are more dejected and disconsolate than saints and believers? Whose lives are more uncomfortable? Whose mouths are more filled with complaints, than theirs? If a condition of godliness and Christianity is a condition of so much comfort, then why are they this way?"

Solution. That the people of God are oftentimes without comfort, I grant, "They may walk in the dark, and have no light." But this is none of the products of godliness. Grace brings forth no such fruit as this; there is a threefold rise and spring of it: sin within, desertion and temptation without.

1. Sin within. The saints of God are not all spirit, and no flesh; all grace, and no sin. They are made up of contrary principles. There is light and darkness in the same mind; sin and grace in the same will; carnal and spiritual in the same affections; there is "the flesh lusting against the Spirit." In all these, and too often the Lord knows, is the believer led away captive by these warring lusts. So was the holy apostle himself, "I find then a Law, that, when I would do good, evil is present with me. I see another Law in my members, warring against the Law of my mind, and bringing me into captivity to the Law of sin," (Romans 7:23), and this was that which broke his spiritual peace, and filled his soul with trouble and complaints, as you see: "O wretched man that I am! who shall deliver me from this body of death?" So that it is sin that interrupts the peace of God's people. Indwelling lust, stirring and breaking forth, must needs cause trouble and grief in the soul of a believer; for it is as natural for sin to bring forth trouble, as it is for grace to bring forth peace. Every sin contracts a new guilt on the soul, and guilt provokes God; and where there is a sense of guilt contracted, and God provoked, there can be no peace, no quiet in that soul, until faith procures fresh sprinklings of the blood of Jesus Christ on the conscience.

2. "Another spring of the believer's trouble and disconsolateness of spirit, is the desertions of God;" and

this follows upon the former. God sometimes disappears, and hides himself from his people. "Verily, you are a God that hideth thyself," (Isa. 45:15). But the cause of God's hiding, is the believer's sinning. "Your iniquities have separated between you and your God, and your sins have hid his face from you." In heaven, where there is no sinning, there is no losing the light of God's countenance for a moment; and if saints here could serve God without corruption, they should enjoy God without desertion; but this cannot be. While we are in this state, remaining lusts will stir and break forth, and then God will hide his face, and this must necessarily create trouble, "Thou didst hide thy face, and I was troubled," (Psa. 30:7).

The light of God's countenance, shining on the soul, is the Christian's heaven on this side heaven; and therefore it is no wonder if the biding of his face be looked on by the soul, as one of the days of hell. So it was by David, "The sorrows of death compassed me, the pains of hell gat hold upon me; I found trouble and sorrow," (Psa. 116:3).

3. "A third spring of that trouble and complaint that brims the banks of the Christian's spirit, is the temptations of Satan." He is the great enemy of saints, and he envies the quiet and comfort that their hearts are filled with, when his conscience is brimmed with horror and terror. And, therefore, though he knows that he cannot destroy their peace, yet he labors to disturb their peace. As the blessed Spirit of God is first a sanctifier, and then a comforter, working grace in order to peace; so this cursed spirit of hell is first a tempter, and then a troubler. He first persuades to act sin, and then accuses for sin; and this is his constant practice on the spirits of God's people. He

cannot endure that they should live in the light of God's countenance, when is himself doomed to eternal, intolerable darkness.

And in this way, you see where it is that the people of God are often under trouble and complaint. All arises from these three springs of sin within, desertions and temptations without.

If the saints could serve God without sinning, and enjoy God without withdrawing, and resist Satan without yielding, they might enjoy peace and comfort without sorrowing. This must be endeavored constantly here, but it will never be attained fully but in heaven. But yet so far as grace is the prevailing principle in the heart, and so far as the power of godliness is exercised in this life; so far the condition of a child of God is a condition of peace; for it is an undoubted truth, that the fruit of righteousness shall be peace. But suppose the people of God experience little of this comfort in this life, *yet*,

2. "They find it in the day of death." Grace and holiness will minister to us then, and that ministration will be peace. A believer has a twofold spring of comfort, each one emptying itself into his soul in a dying season; one is from above him, the other is from within him. The spring that runs comfort from above him, is the blood of Christ sprinkled on the conscience; the spring that runs comfort from within him, is the sincerity of his heart in God's service. When we lie on a death-bed, and can reflect on our principles and performances in the service of God, and there find uprightness and sincerity of heart running through all, this must needs be comfort. It was so to Hezekiah, "Remember, O Lord, how I have walked before

thee in truth, and with a perfect heart; and have done that which is good in thy sight," (2 Kings 20:3).

Nothing makes a death-bed so uneasy and hard, as a life spent in the service of sin and lust; nothing makes a death-bed so soft and sweet, as a life spent in the service of God and Christ. Or put the case, the people of God should not meet with this comfort then; *yet*,

3. "They shall be sure to find it after death." If time brings none of this fruit to ripeness, yet eternity shall; grace in time will be glory in eternity; holiness now will be happiness then. "Whatever it is a man soweth in this world, that he shall be sure to reap in the next world: he that soweth to the flesh shall of the flesh reap corruption: but he that soweth to the spirit, shall of the spirit reap life everlasting," (Gal. 6:8). When sin shall end in sorrow and misery, holiness shall end in joy and glory, "Well done, thou good and faithful servant, enter thou into the joy of thy Lord," (Matthew 25:23). Whoever shares in the grace of Christ in this world, shall share in the joys of Christ in the world to come; and that joy "is joy unspeakable, and full of glory." Lo, here is the fruit of godliness. Tell me now if there is not enough in religion, whether we respect profit or comfort, to engage us to be Christians throughout?

CONSIDERATION 4. "What an entire resignation wicked men make of themselves to their lusts! and shall not we do so to the Lord Christ?" They give up themselves without reserve to the pleasures of sin; and shall we have our reserves in the service of God? They are altogether sinners; and shall not we be altogether saints? They run, and do not faint in the service of their lusts; and shall we faint, and not run, in the service of Christ? Shall the servants of corruption have their ears bored to the doorposts of sin, in token of an entire and perpetual service, and shall we not give up ourselves to the Lord Christ, to be his forever? Shall others make a "covenant with hell and death," and shall not we "join ourselves to God in an everlasting covenant that cannot be forgotten?" Shall they take more pains to damn their souls, than we do to save ours, and make more speed to a place of vengeance, than we do to a crown of righteousness? Which do you judge best, to be saved everlastingly, or to perish everlastingly? Which do you count the best master, God or the devil? Christ or your lusts? I know you will determine it on Christ's side. O then! when others serve their lusts with all their hearts, do you serve Christ with all your hearts? If the hearts of the sons of men are fully set in them to do evil, then much more let the hearts of the sons of God be fully set in them to do good.

CONSIDERATION 5. "If you are not altogether Christians, you will never be able to appear with comfort before God, nor to stand in the judgment of the last and great day." For this sad dilemma will silence every hypocrite. If my commands were not holy, just, and good, why did you own them? If they were holy, just, and good, why do you not obey them? If Jesus Christ was not worth having, why did you profess him? If he was, then why did you not cleave to him, and close with him? If my ordinances were not appointed to convert and save souls, why did you sit under them, and rest in their performance? Or if they were, then why did you not submit to their power? If religion is not good, why do you profess it? If it is good, why do you not practice it? "Friend, how earnest thou in hither, not having on a wedding garment?" (Matthew 22:12). If it was not a wedding-feast, why did you come at the invitation? If it was, then why did you come without a wedding garment?

I would but ask a hypocritical professor of the Gospel, what he will answer in that day? Truly you deprive yourselves of all possibility of apology in "the day of the righteous judgment of God." It is said of the man that had no wedding garment on, that when Christ came and examined him, he was *speechless*. He that is graceless in a day of grace, will be speechless in a day of judgment. Professing Christ without a heart to close with Christ, will leave our souls inexcusable, and make our damnation unavoidable and more intolerable.

These are the motives to enforce the duty; and O that God would set them home upon your hearts and consciences, that you might not dare to rest a moment longer in a half-work, or in being Christians within a little, but that you might be altogether Christians!

QUESTION. But you will say possibly, "How shall I do? What means shall I use, that I may attain to a thorough work in my heart, that I may be no longer almost, but altogether a Christian?"

Answer. Now I shall lay down three rules of direction instead of many, to further and help you in this important duty, and so leave this work to God's blessing.

DIRECTION 1. "Break off all false peace of conscience;" this is the devil's bond to hold the soul from seeking after Christ. As there is the peace of God so there is the peace of Satan; but they are easily known, for they are as contrary as heaven and hell, as light and darkness.

The peace of God flows from a work of grace in the soul, and is the peace of a regenerate state; but the peace of Satan is the peace of an unregenerate state, it is the peace of death; in the grave Job says there is peace, "There the wicked cease from troubling," (Job 3:17), so a soul dead in sin is full of peace, the wicked one does not trouble him. The peace of God in the soul is a peace flowing from removal of guilt, by justifying grace. "Being justified by faith in his blood, we have peace with God," (Romans 5:1), but the peace of Satan in the soul arises and is maintained by a stupidity of spirit, and insensibility of guilt upon the conscience. The peace of God is a peace from sin that fortifies the heart against it. "The peace of God that passeth all men's understanding, shall, keep your hearts and minds through Christ Jesus," (Phil. 4:7). The more of this peace there is in the soul, the more is the soul fortified against sin; but the peace of Satan is peace in sin, "The strong man armed keeps the house, and there is all at peace," (Luke 11:21). The saint's peace is a peace with God, but not with sin; the sinner's peace is a peace with sin, but not with God. And this is a peace better broken than kept. It is a false, a dangerous, an undoing peace. My brethren, death and judgment will break all peace of conscience, but not that which is fashioned by Christ in the soul, and is the fruit of the "blood of sprinkling." "When he gives quietness, who can make trouble?" (Job 34:29). Now that peace that death will break, why should you keep? Who would be fond of that quietness which the flames of hell will burn in sunder? And yet how many travel to hell through the fool's paradise of a false peace? O break off this peace! For we can have no peace with God in Christ, while this peace remains in our hearts. The Lord Christ gives no peace to them that will not seek it; and that man will never seek it that does not see his need of it; and he that is at peace in his lusts sees no need of the peace of Christ. The sinner must be wounded for sin, and troubled under it, before Christ will heal his wounds, and give him peace from it.

DIRECTION 2. Labor after a thorough work of conviction; every conviction will not do it. The almost Christian has his convictions as well as the true Christian, or else he had never gone so far; but they are not sound and right convictions, or else he would have gone further. God will have the soul truly sensible of the bitterness of sin before it shall taste the sweetness of mercy. The plough of conviction must go deep, and make deep furrows in the heart, before God will sow the precious seed of grace and comfort there, so that it may have depth of earth to grow in. This is the constant method of God. First, to show man his sin, then his Savior; first his danger, then his Redeemer; first his wound, then his cure; first his own vileness, then Christ's righteousness. We must be brought to cry out, "Unclean, unclean!" to mourn for Him whom we have pierced, and then he sets open for us a fountain to wash in for sin, and for uncleanness. That is a notable place, Job 33:27-28. "He looked upon men; and if any say, I have sinned, and perverted that which was right, and it profited me not; he will deliver his soul from going into the pit, and his life shall see the light." The sinner must see the unprofitableness of his unrighteousness, before he profits by Christ's righteousness. The Israelites are first stung with the fiery serpents, and then the brazen serpent is set up. Ephraim is first thoroughly convinced, and then God's bowels of mercy worked toward him. It was in this way with Paul, Manasseh, the jailer, *etc.* So that this is the unchangeable method of God in working grace, to begin with conviction of sin. O! therefore labor for thorough conviction; and there are three things we should especially be convinced of.

First, be convinced of the evil of sin; its filthy and heinous nature. This is the greatest evil in the world; it wrongs God, it wounds Christ, it grieves the Holy Spirit, it ruins a precious soul; all other evils are not to be named with this. My brethren, though to do sin is the worst work, yet to see sin is the best sight; for sin discovered in its vileness, makes Christ to be desired in his fulness. But above all, labor to be convinced of the mischief of an unsound heart; what an abhorrence it is to God, what certain ruin it brings on the soul. O think often on the hypocrite's hell. "For this people's heart is waxed gross, and their ears are dull of hearing, and their eyes they have closed; lest at any time they should see with their eyes, and hear with their ears, and should understand with their heart, and should be converted, and I should heal them," (Matthew 13:15 and Acts 28:27).

Secondly, be convinced of the misery and desperate danger of a natural condition; for until we see the plague of our hearts and the misery of our state by nature, we shall never be brought off ourselves to seek help in another.

Thirdly, be convinced of the utter insufficiency and inability of anything below Christ Jesus to minister relief to your soul in this case. All things besides Jesus Christ are "physicians of no value;" duties, performances, prayers, tears, self-righteousness, avail nothing in this case; they make us like the troops of Tema, to return "ashamed at our disappointment" from such "failing brooks."

Alas! it is an infinite righteousness that must satisfy for us, for it is an infinite God that is offended by us. If ever your sin is to be pardoned, it is infinite mercy that must pardon it; if ever you are to be reconciled to God, it is infinite merit that must do it. If ever your heart is to be changed, and your state renewed, it is infinite power that must effect it; and if ever your soul is to escape hell, and be saved at last, it is infinite grace that must save it.

In these three things right and sound conviction lies. And wherever the Spirit of God works these thorough convictions, it is in order to a true and sound conversion. For by this means the soul is brought under a right qualification for receiving Christ.

You must know; that a sinner can never come to Christ; for he is dead in sin, in enmity against Christ, an enemy to God, and the grace of God; but there are certain qualifications that come between the soul's dead state in sin, and the work of conversion and closing with Christ, by which the soul is put into a capacity of receiving the Lord Jesus Christ. For, no man is brought immediately out of his dead state and made to believe in Jesus Christ; there are some qualifications coming in between. Now sound convictions are the right qualifications for the sinner's receiving Christ, "for he came not to call the righteous, but sinners to repentance;" that is, such as see themselves sinners, and by this are in a lost condition. So, Luke exemplifies it, "The Son of Man is come to seek and to save that which was lost," (Luke 19:10). "He is anointed, and sent to bind up the brokenhearted," (Isa. 61:1), to comfort all that mourn.

O! therefore, if you would be sound Christians, get sound convictions; ask those that are believers indeed, and they will tell you, had it not been for their convictions, they would never have sought after Christ for sanctification and salvation. They will tell you they would have perished; they would have been in eternal bondage in the life to come. Yet, because God opened their eyes and they saw their spiritual bondage, they saw their need of Christ, and so they saw they were lost as to Christ, and needed to be saved by him.

DIRECTION 3. Never rest in convictions until they end in conversion. This is that in which most men miscarry. They rest in their convictions, and take them for conversion, as if sin seen were therefore forgiven, as if a sight of the need of grace were the truth of the work of grace.

That is a notable place in Hosea 13:13, "Ephraim is an unwise son, for he should not stay long in the place of the breaking forth of children." The place of breaking forth of children is the womb; as the child comes out of the womb, so is conversion born out of the womb of conviction. Now when the child sticks between the womb and the world, it is dangerous, it hazards the life both of mother and child. So, when a sinner rests in conviction, and goes no farther, but sticks "in the place of the breaking forth of children," this is very dangerous and hazards the life of the soul.

You that are at any time under convictions, O take heed of resting in them, do not stay long in the place of the breaking forth of children: though it is true, that conviction is the first step to conversion, yet it is not conversion; a man may carry his convictions along with him into hell.

What is that which troubles poor creatures, when they come to die, but this; I have not improved my convictions at such a time I was convinced of sin, but yet I went on in sin in the face of my convictions. In such a sermon I was convinced of such a duty, but I slighted the conviction; I was convinced of my need of Christ, and of the readiness of Christ to pardon and save. But, alas! I did not follow the conviction.

My brethren, remember this, slighted convictions are the worst death bed companions. There are two things especially, which above all others, make a death bed very uncomfortable:

1. Purposes and promises not performed.
2. Convictions slighted and not improved.

This is when a man takes up purposes to close with Christ, and yet does not put them into execution. And when he is convinced of sin and duty, and yet does not improve his convictions, O this will sting and wound at last.

Now therefore, has the Spirit of the Lord been at work in your souls? Have you ever been convinced of the evil of sin, of the misery of a natural state, of the insufficiency of all things under heaven to help, of the fullness and righteousness of Jesus Christ, of the necessity of resting on him for pardon and peace, for sanctification and salvation? Have you ever been really convinced of these things? O then, as you love your own souls, as ever

Use of Exhortation

you hope to be saved at last, and enjoy God forever, improve these convictions, and be sure you do not rest in them until they rise up to a thorough close with the Lord Jesus Christ, and so end in a sound and perfect conversion. In this way shall you be not only *almost*, but *altogether a Christian*.

FINIS

Other Helpful Works by Matthew Mead at Puritan Publications

The Danger of Falling into the Hands of the Living God
by Matthew Mead (1630-1699)
> There will be a day when saints and sinners will both fall into the hands of the Living God. On such a day, judgment will occur. Are you ready? This masterful exposition of Hebrews 10:31 (and part of Chapter 4) by Matthew Mead is one of the most powerful works on the God with whom we are to deal on the Day of Judgment.

Discovering the Wickedness of Our Heart
by Matthew Mead (1630-1699)
> Do you know the depth of the wickedness of your heart? Few Puritan works dive headlong into such deep waters as this work by Matthew Mead. Mead was present at the plague in London, and uses the means of that horrifying time to press sinners to repent, and cause Christians to wake up out of their lethargy. This is a powerful exhortation for one of the best puritan preachers of the day.

The Christian's Duty to Walk Wisely
by Matthew Mead (1630-1699)
> This is, no doubt, one of the best works we've ever published. In a simple and easy to follow manner, in two parts, Mead teaches Christians how to fight against Satan's temptations, and walk wisely in the trials that come to them from God. Secondly, he also shows the Christian how to love Christ more, and love the world less. This is a rare puritan work, and ought to be required reading for every Christian who desires to combat the world, the flesh and devil so that they might walk wisely before God.

The Vision of the Wheels: A Treatise on the Providence of God
by Matthew Mead (1630-1699)
> One of the editors said, "This is, no doubt, one of the best books on the biblical doctrine of God's providence I've ever read." Matthew Mead's treatment of Ezekiel's wheels is astounding, poignant and powerful. This is a book on providence that should not be missed.

www.ingramcontent.com/pod-product-compliance
Lightning Source LLC
LaVergne TN
LVHW041542070426
835507LV00011B/880